Priesthood in Reality

LIVING THE VOCATION OF A DIOCESAN PRIEST
IN A CHANGING WORLD

Tony Philpot

First published in 1998 by
KEVIN MAYHEW LTD
Rattlesden
Bury St Edmunds
Suffolk IP30 0SZ

0 1 2 3 4 5 6 7 8 9

ISBN 1 84003 147 6
Catalogue No 1500166

Cover illustration: Paper Collage by Bettina Healey
Cover design by Jaquetta Sergeant
Typesetting by Louise Hill
Printed and bound in Great Britain

CONTENTS

INTRODUCTION

This book began as a reflection on the identity of the diocesan priest in the Catholic Church. The diocesan priest is, so to speak, a unique character in the Church, his vocation has a particular taste and flavour to it. I have not found this taste and flavour adequately described anywhere, and I wanted to sum it up in a way which would enable men to say, 'Yes, that's how it is. I recognise myself in that picture.'

A question is often asked about the spirituality most suitable for the diocesan priest. Is this question really about the pattern of prayer best adapted to life in a presbytery? Well, I think that if it's about formal prayer (when, for how long, content), it's the wrong question. Spirituality adds up to more than this. More than alternative methods and routines. Your spirituality is how you live your life, in what spirit you live your life, with what motivation you live your life, with what hope and faith you live your life. It isn't *apart* from life. It isn't even apart from the lives of those you serve. My relationship with God, what I want to say to God, the questions I ask God, are nearly all earthed in the place where I work and the people I serve. The real question is 'How can I pray my way through the events of my private and professional life, so that nothing and no one is left outside the ambit of God's love and mercy?' And, secondly, 'How do I resource myself for this life?' Georges Gilson, a French bishop writing for the priests of his diocese in the late 1980s, said that the best spiritual reading book for the diocesan priest is his diary. That brought me up short when I read it. It still does.

It is true that the diocesan priest has no vow of poverty, or chastity, or obedience. He makes some promises, that is true, incurs some obligations. But if there is a force which makes him unextravagant, or chaste, or obedient, it is his own maturity, and generosity, and his sense of what the job demands. He is thrown back on his own resources. To a large extent he has to pioneer his own spiritual way, and set his own standards. The specific spirituality of the diocesan priest *is* this mixture of maturity, and generosity, and awareness. I wanted to explore this. I wanted to examine how time generously given to prayer fits into a busy and interrupted life, full of the unpredictable. I wanted to think about the tangled skein of relationships which are also part of that spirituality – relationships with superiors, with other clergy, with parishioners. Nobody seeks holiness in a vacuum. I wanted to think of the peculiar challenges of living alone, and of being largely – in the professional sense – unsupervised. So I started this book.

Halfway through writing it, I heard that I was to be involved, at one remove, with a seminary. This, immediately, sharpened the focus. What would I want students to know about the life on which they were embarking? Some things can't be explained in advance; you have to live them to understand them. But other things can be spelled out, or at least hinted at. I thought back to my own student days, and what we were *not* told, largely because those who should have told us were themselves academics, or had been too long away from the coalface of parish or diocesan life. I emerged from the seminary, in the late 1950s, with principles sticking out all over me like a porcupine's quills, well equipped with undigested theology but distinctly short on common sense. I remember being asked at short notice to look after the local branch of the Catholic Nurses' Guild, just for an evening. They were lovely, those nurses, many of them recently over from Ireland, living a gruesome military regime up at the General Hospital, and desperately in need of some sympathy and friendship. Unfortunately I wasn't their man. I was still hooked on the books and insensitive to people. I gave them a half-hour lecture on 'The Structure of the Act of Faith'. At bad moments, even now, when I wake at two in the morning, racked with shame, I can see their glazed expressions. They must be grandmothers approaching sixty by now. Wherever they are, I hope they forgive me.

How can I help the men approaching ordination not to be like me?

There were some things I just wasn't ready for, when I arrived on a hot August afternoon at my first presbytery. The parish priest and the other curate were having tea. There was no rapturous welcome and there were no speeches. Instead, they said, 'Oh, good – you've come. That leaves us free to go out.' It was my first intimation that I was not the centre of the known world and the answer to all the Catholic Church's longings. Here are a few more of the things I had still to discover.

The diocesan priest is a private man. There is an area of his life to which very few people have access. This is the area of his own faith and convictions, what really makes him tick. Self-disclosure comes hard. So there isn't much sharing in presbyteries. The ethos of the British male doesn't exactly encourage it. In addition to which, does the determination to live a celibate life mean, in practice, a determined 'No' to intimacy of any kind? It shouldn't, but sometimes it does.

The diocesan priest is the custodian of other people's secrets. Some of these are confessional matter, but most of them are not. He knows things, in a privileged way, about the people in his parish and sometimes, too, about his brother priests. Secrets can be a heavy load to bear. This can be where loneliness bites.

The diocesan priest is, as a rule, genuinely classless. Of course there are exceptions to this, where a man cannot prescind from his own background and finds it hard to mix with those who don't share it. But this is unusual. Most Catholics will like one priest more than another, but this liking and disliking spans the barriers of accent and education. Nationality, too. It's the fact of priesthood which makes us acceptable wherever we go, *what* we are rather than *who* we are.

The diocesan priest is magisterial. He may speak in a liberated way, but at the same time he is profoundly aware of the authority-structure of the Church. He may talk brave talk about collaborative ministry, and, if he is wise, go a long way in sharing and delegating responsibility. But in the final analysis he is conscious that he is answerable to the Bishop for what happens on his patch. The same magisterial instinct is present in the pulpit. He expects to be listened to, not argued with, when holding forth and preaching the Gospel. It gets more difficult when the holding-forth is done, not in church, but in a school hall or a meeting room. Here he is liable to meet respectful hecklers, and occasionally checkers-up with clipboards who make notes while he speaks, implying that a report will be forwarded to some unnamed potentate afterwards. Some priests are experts in dealing with this silken kind of criticism and keep their cool. Some find it hard to take. Knowing how to keep your cool is vital.

The diocesan priest has to talk, far too often, about sacred things. He is taught at the seminary to prepare his Sunday homily well in advance, to study the scripture of the Mass, pray about it, read round it, apply it to current events. But in the course of the week he will also be called upon to officiate at a funeral (with a homily), celebrate a nuptial Mass (with a homily), baptise a baby (with a homily), speak at the R.C.I.A. or equivalent 'journey in faith' for new arrivals, appear at a school assembly and speak off the cuff to the children, hear some confessions where the words need to be incisive, encouraging and lastingly helpful – and all this within the space of seven days. Every time he opens his mouth he is dealing with the eternal, the absolute, matters of spiritual life and death, nothing trivial, everything important. How do you learn to think on your feet? To be flexible and quick off the mark? How do you avoid going on to automatic pilot, repeating things endlessly, and giving the impression that you don't really believe what you are saying?

The diocesan priest deals, *ex professo*, with failure. There is, of course, his own failure, the knowledge of his own sinfulness. But there is also the fact that the Gospel is about the forgiveness of sins, and his vocation is to deal with the sins of his flock. To help them advert to what is corrupt in their own lives and in society. To help them repent, so that God may forgive them. Failure is the raw material on which he works. He is aware, for instance, that the majority of his youngsters are cohabiting, many without the slightest intention of getting married. He can point out the houses where there is a massive problem of alcoholism, or drug abuse, or tax avoidance on a truly noble scale. He knows the families where quite small children are having their brains addled by unhealthy videos, night after night. He lives at the centre of communities of great moral turbulence, where many folk are struggling, and not winning. He knows that, in the face of this ethical wasteland, he is relatively ineffective, and regarded as irrelevant. He dwells with imperfection, lives with failure.

At the same time the diocesan priest is the witness to great and miraculous joy among ordinary people. It may be about trivial things, or awesome ones. He can be the middleman who puts the family with a Christmas turkey too many in touch with the family which is going without, and who handles it tactfully so that no one feels patronised. He shares the delight of the mother and father of a baby which is born, against all odds, healthy and thriving. Of an out-of-work youngster who successfully carves himself a new furrow. Of the man or woman without faith who comes to the R.C.I.A. and, a third of the way into it, has a Road to Damascus experience. Of the Catholic who has been away from the Church for ages, and who comes to confession, and is moved to tears with sheer relief and happiness. Of the dying patient in hospital who is anointed, and finds peace, and is able to say his 'Nunc Dimittis' at last. He is the midwife to some of the most profound things in human existence. And all these things can happen within weeks of ordination.

Some diocesan priests are spick and span, impressive in their blackness and whiteness. Others, in stained anoraks and dusty boots, and badly needing haircuts, seem at first sight more like brush salesmen. Some are professorial in their manner, and some frankly entrepreneurial. It honestly doesn't matter. What matters is that all, or nearly all, have acquired a street-wisdom which is more valuable than a clutch of degrees. A surprising unshockability. A sureness of touch in dealing with the recesses of the human heart. A nose for what is phoney, fake and pretentious. An instinct for what is genuine, and real, and substantial. An absence of sentimentality, a refusal to turn human drama into soap-opera. This unspectacular matter-of-factness can seem drab; in reality it is one of our greatest strengths.

The diocesan priest has to learn to live without affirmation. There are few bouquets handed out from Bishop's House. When you are just ordained, the parish priest is vastly relieved if you are punctual and civil to the parishioners, and may call you to order if you're not. Apart from that, he will leave you more alone than you like, because he has his own agenda to get through, and isn't very good at accompanying beginners. You will find that, on the whole, people are not as excited by your recent ordination as you are. They accept your prayer-card politely, but their minds are elsewhere. You will gradually realise that you are being taken for granted. This does not mean the same as 'not appreciated'. It means that you are perceived as a priest among other priests, and that, in fact, is good. When, however, you feel too little supported in your ministry, you should ask whether you yourself are good at affirming other priests. We can be a bit dour with one another, enquire too infrequently, be grudging with praise.

The diocesan priest realises pretty soon that the areas of justice and peace, and of ecumenism, while powerfully present in the Council decrees, are in practice marginal in many parishes. There are unspoken blocks. Some priests frankly lack any fellow-feeling with other Christian traditions, and lack sympathy, too, for the poor of the Third World. Soon after your ordination, you may discover that you are the only man in the presbytery who takes these issues seriously. On the other hand, you may find you are fed to a parish priest who hails from the 1960s and is committed very deeply to these things, while you look on from the touchline and conclude that he's making a lot of noise but going nowhere, and that he is neglecting the really important questions of doctrinal orthodoxy, liturgical correctness and thorough catechesis. In other words, within the unity of the Church, people's hearts are in different places. You will be tempted to embark on a corrective mission, and impose your own point of view. Be careful. Get some experience under your belt before setting out your stall as a reformer, in whatever direction.

The diocesan priest starts his ministry with others, but sees on the near horizon the prospect of living by himself. He looks around the diocese and sees men who cope with this in different ways. Some live neat and tidy lives, eat properly, furnish their houses tastefully, keep the place clean, are methodical. Some live in one room, seldom take their coat off when they come in, tend to dine out of tins, and do the washing-up when there are no clean plates left. Some invite the parishioners into their house and share it with them, to the point where they seem to have no territory of their own at all. Some pull down the portcullis from the first day, hoist the drawbridge, and make statements about their Need for Privacy and Space. Some are hospitable to other priests, and some are recluses. Some answer the phone; some leave the answering machine on all day, and don't pick up the messages. If he is wise, a new priest will learn from other people's mistakes, take note, and plan his own pattern of life. What does it mean to live in a house by yourself? What signal does it give, if by your teaching you're encouraging people to join the community of the Church and play their part in it? Is your house the enclosed place where you watch television, or is it your power-base where you can enrich friends and are enriched by them?

Some of these questions I shall try, if not to answer, at least to ventilate.

The Catholic Church has never lacked great and towering

personalities. They may be cardinals, or missionaries, or head teachers, or visionary writers on the contemplative life. Whatever they are now, once they were ordinary parishioners. The odds are that the priest they first knew, and who had the most formative effect upon them, was a diocesan priest. Diocesan priests provide the seedbed from which so many other good things spring. That is why their specific spirituality is worth discussing.

CHAPTER 1

Calling in the falcon

I went to a village agricultural show in Derbyshire, on a very hot August morning. At the show there was a falconer. He released his birds and they flew straight up into the sky, and away. Then he called to them with a weird throaty cry, and whirled some rabbit skin on the end of a cord. In they came, swooping over the trees with utter accuracy, dropping out of the blue like stones. From nowhere they seemed to come, and just as quickly they disappeared again. Towards the end of the afternoon the male bird got lost, and we wondered whether he had seized his chance of freedom, or was hunting fat pigeons far off in the Peaks. The falconer was unworried. 'He'll come,' he said, and started to pack his gear away in his van. And sure enough, half an hour later he did, skimming the tops of the tall beeches and limes round the village green, poising himself on a thermal and circling round, relaxing, then diving in for his supper. There was a complicity between him and the falconer. They knew one another's ways.

For me this provides an analogy which is clear, and helpful. God is the God who comes. He lives in a dimension I cannot control or even comprehend. It is above me and beyond me. But if I call, and am patient, he comes. He comes on his own terms, and I must accept those terms and submit to them. Yet in another way he makes himself my captive. There is complicity between us. I have (it brings the heart into the mouth to say this) not so much captured him as captivated him. He loves me. He has invested so much in me. He cannot not come, when I call. ('My Father and I will come to him, and live with him.' John 14:23) I have nothing with which to tempt him. No spiritual bribe, like the rabbit-skin on the end of the cord. What brings him in is my lovability, which he put into me when he created me, making me in his own image and likeness, and again when he adopted me at Baptism. No credit to me: I neither conceived nor baptised myself. And even now I cannot claim any credit. I can only be who I am in the presence of God, allowing him to love me for his own reasons, and rejoicing that I am loved, and doing my feeble best to love in return. The point is that his coming is gratuitous, not bought. All I have to do, and all I can do, is ask, and believe, and wait.

So when I pray I don't have to do much. This is not the time or the place for logic, or theology. It is a time and place for idling and dawdling, but idling and dawdling in an alert way, aware of God, wanting him, keeping the door open to him, welcoming him. Asking, believing and waiting. St John of the Cross, in his poem *The Dark Night*, describes the search of the soul for God: 'Ni yo miraba cosa, sin otra luz y guía, sino la que en el corazón ardía.' 'I didn't look at anything else, and my only light and guide was the one which burned in my heart.' In other words, wanting is enough. Do I want sufficiently? This is what St John of the Cross would ask me. Not if I am diligent enough when I pray, neat enough, tidy enough, organised enough: but whether I want sufficiently.

Do I want, to such an extent, that I am prepared to pray without fail every day? I don't mean to be fundamentalist about this; there will always be exceptional days. But how much of a priority is this for me? There are times when the falcon circles and circles above the trees, and night draws on, and there is no call. This is my tragedy, that I am too laid-back by half about my spiritual life, and I play fast and loose with God, and in human terms I deserve to lose him. As a diocesan priest I can find a dozen alibis, things to prepare, people to visit, letters to write. Sometimes these things are just like wayward ponies in a gymkhana. They dominate me. They need pulling into line. I can, of course, persuade myself that I find God in these things and these people, that they are part of my prayer. Indeed, this is true; I cannot exclude them from my prayer. But they are not a replacement for prayer. And for them to be part of it, I have to carve out an inviolable place in my life where prayer will actually happen. Still the falcon circles in the failing light, listening for the call. If I provide no space for him to land, he cannot come.

God is the God who comes. He is also the God who is here already.

We believe that he dwells within us. St Teresa of Avila describes this graphically in *The Interior Castle*. In a Renaissance castle there's a moat, and there are outer ramparts, and courtyards, and buildings of all kinds. But the chief place, the impregnable place, the non-negotiable place is the keep, the central tower, right at the heart of the whole complex. If you think of your soul as a castle, well, the Lord lives in the keep. If the keep is the heart of a castle, in the same way this part of my soul is the quintessence of me, the 'me-ness' of me, the most authentic part of me, where my character and most fundamental attitudes and convictions have their origin.

When I was baptised I was too young to be complicated. My identity was simple and unsullied. I was like a tiny sapling planted in good soil. At this point, by Baptism, the Lord came and entwined himself in my infant roots. Inextricably he involved himself with me. He was so much 'in at the start of me' that however much I shoot up, develop, become sophisticated, become learned, become famous, grow away from my first beginnings, he will always be there at the root of me.

Institutions and businesses have 'mission statements', short declarations which sum up their *raison d'être*, and which govern all their later choices of aims and objectives. The mission statement of my life is in the roots of the sapling; it is in the keep of the castle. It is so hard of access that I may never have discovered it. Perhaps I've never been there, never dug down to the roots, never pushed open the final door. But it's there, the answer to the question 'What makes me tick?' Maybe one day I will find that mission statement, and solve, for myself, the enigma of my own existence. This much I do know, even now: that ever since my Baptism, the living Lord has been there in the roots, in the keep, and my personal mission statement must include mention of him. He is indissolubly part of my deepest identity. ('I live, now not I, but God lives in me.' Galatians 2:20.)

So I am a living tabernacle, a walking Ark of the Covenant, and when I want to worship God I find him, obscurely but certainly, here.

Only in the soul of the baptised? Surely not. It is not my job to shorten the arm of the Lord, and say that he does not make a similar arrangement for Jews and Muslims, and for all those whom the Second Vatican Council recognised and saluted as living by the light they were given. I am not trying to create a Christian corral. All I am saying is this: that for us, the moment of our Baptism is a decisive one.

Now, I am not so much living on borrowed time as on borrowed premises, for I am on God's property, formally made over to him. The castle keep is his. It is the place where he allows me to live in communion with him, knowing and being known. Over the sacristy door in a Polish village church, I once saw an old picture of a triangle containing an eye. It was a 17th-century image of the Holy Trinity, three-in-one, and the eye was saying to the folk in church, 'Look out, because I can see you, and everything you do.' Anything with just one eye I find sinister; it reminds me of the Cyclops, or of something out of science fiction. When I saw this one, however, it struck me that the eye has another meaning, which is not surveillance, but recognition. How much expression eyes can carry, even at a first glance! I can cull from the look in your eyes that, while you wish to be polite, you are bored stiff with my company. I can realise in a split second that, although a complete stranger, you are at this moment in need of an outsize dose of sympathy. I can know with near-certainty that, even if this is our first meeting, you would quite like to press home the friendship. I can tell from your clouded and abstracted eye that you are in trouble, and too full of your own concerns to have time for anyone else. Eyes are the agents of mutual recognition and appreciation between people. Well, the keep of the castle is the place in which God and I recognise one another. It is the place where eyes meet, where I can know and be known. This, too, is a 'given'. I do not have to create it, or invent it, or imagine it, or work at it. I simply have to accept it. The place where I am most at home is the place where I cohabit with the Lord of the Universe, who is also Lord of the human psyche.

The algebra I learned in the 1940s had little, so it seemed, to do with real life. It felt like a series of arbitrary hurdles erected by sadistic schoolmasters. I knocked the hurdles over, mostly. But one thing I do remember, and that is The Bracket. You could put an expression (for example, 'x plus y plus z') inside a bracket; and outside you could put a number; and the number influenced everything within the bracket. $3(x + y + z)$ meant $3x + 3y + 3z$.

When we pray, whether we are calling in the falcon or retreating into the keep, the example holds. If I begin my prayer with a positive statement – of faith, of need, of sorrow for sin, of thanksgiving, of love – that's like putting the number outside the bracket. Having done it, I can forget about it. That intention will be present in all my prayer, on this occasion. I may spend the time simply 'being' in God's presence. I may get distracted. I may go to sleep. I may plough doggedly on, seeking the face of the Lord and apparently not finding him. Or I may quickly achieve a peaceful sense of being with him, being the disciple at his feet, being Nicodemus at his house, being Zacchaeus with him in mine. It honestly doesn't much matter. The overall intention, made and shelved, affects everything that happens, gives it the value of, at least, a gallant effort. And gallant efforts are the currency of the kingdom.

What I have written in this chapter is true and necessary for every Christian. Personal prayer is not a clerical preserve. But when I think, with affection, of diocesan priests throughout the world, it seems to me that this is a particular need and priority for them. Why? Because they have to teach other people to pray, teach them that it isn't hard, teach them not to be afraid. Every contemplative monk or sister began to know the Lord in a parish, after all, and their first guide was most probably a diocesan priest. Diocesan priests are in more intimate contact than anyone I know with the broad mass of Catholics. The signals they put out are influential, formative. If they are perceived mainly as curators of church buildings, then the parishioners will express their loyalty to the Church through fundraising. If they are perceived as organisers of the liturgy, then the parishioners will form choirs, and train better readers and eucharistic ministers. If they are seen as, above all, promoters of Catholic education, then some of the parishioners at least will rally round the parish school and support it. All of these things are vital. I've done them, or tried to do them, all myself. Parishes don't survive unless they are in place. Crumbling churches, chaotic worship and under-supported schools are bad news.

But even with public worship and the fabric and the upbringing of the children in fine fettle, there is still something missing. 'Mary has chosen the better part, and it shall not be taken from her' (Luke 10:42). What matters most is communion with the God we cannot see; all else is a means to this end.

As a diocesan priest I am a witness to this. My vocation is to be a witness. To speak to people about the Father, and my experience of him, which is always fresh and always new. If I do this I am actually on a journey of faith with the people. I am not the all-knowing and paternalistic manipulator of the flock, or administrator of a sure-fire system. I am a brother of Christ on the way home to the Father, able sometimes to point the way to others, and not above being helped by them. Personal prayer puts me on this journey. Whether in front of the Eucharist in the monstrance or tabernacle, or sitting in my room with the Gospels, retreating into my castle keep and shutting the door for a while, or patiently calling the falcon home, this is the central stuff of my vocation as a priest of my diocese.

CHAPTER 2

Liturgy

Priests as old as I am have had to learn the difference between liturgy and rubrics. We were brought up on a hard assault course, covered with thickets of prescriptive-laws-binding under-sin. You could get badly scratched in those thickets. Some men became neurotic, twitchy and scrupulous, and worried themselves sick about candles which blew out in draughty convent chapels, words in the breviary glossed over, and Latin words improperly pronounced at key moments of the Mass. These things are amusing to think about now; at the time they were painful, and tragic. It is surprising that we retained any feeling for the Church at worship, for the broad, majestic flow and movement of the liturgy. For those ordained in the 1950s or before, therefore, the Council was a great time of learning and discovering. We had to adapt on the hoof. And we had to leave a lot of baggage behind. Some of us managed better than others. There was no lengthy in-service re-training for us diocesan clergy, because – allegedly – there wasn't time and the men could not be spared away from their parishes. Younger priests fared better, because the seminaries began to take liturgy very seriously, and from the '60s on it became a major subject.

The result is that today liturgy can be a very inflammable topic. It arouses fierce passions in the clerical breast. It can poison relationships in presbyteries. When liturgy begins to be discussed, many of us have nerves which stick out like stalks. On the sanctuary a man who is normally agreeable and approachable can become a tough dictator, a tyrant impatient with bumblers. It can, on the other hand, be a creative and beautiful structure in men's lives, bringing harmony into what would otherwise be chaotic, and giving them a priceless way of leading the people at the Eucharist and in prayer, a way which is real, dignified, purposeful, and, thank God, not invented on the spot.

The liturgy offers the same consolation as a moving train. Few of us would make much of a job of driving a train, especially first thing in the morning, but most of us could manage to jump on, so long as it was not travelling too fast. Since the liturgy is the prayer of the whole Church, it is in progress even as we prepare to start the psalms, or approach the altar for Mass: it is already going on, the train is already in motion, and we do not have to drive the train. We simply contribute our voice to the chorus.

The pre-conciliar Church used to thrive on feasts and special celebrations. The calendar was full of events, and in Catholic countries the town band would be enlisted with the erratic drum and the off-beat tuba, and the hangings and the bunting were produced and draped across the road like really exciting washing, and the heaviest cope and the most embroidered canopy were put to use, not once but many times a year. What the Council did was introduce us to the beauty of what is ordinary, and simple, sometimes even a little stark. The beauty of an uneventful green Sunday of the Year. The simple dignity of a ferial Mass, with two substantial pieces of Scripture to reflect upon, an unhurried eucharistic prayer, a quiet time after communion, a simple dismissal without volumes of notices. For some people the self-discipline of the Church, cutting down the number of obligatory saints' days and allowing the seasons to re-emerge, was distressing. For most of us, I think, it was a relief.

But hot on the heels of the Saints came the Themes. These are still with us, and are sometimes harder to deal with. World Peace, Christian Unity, Education Sunday, World Day of Prayer for the Sick, Family Fast, Vocations Day, Day of Prayer for God's Blessing on Human Work ('Productive Land in rural areas'), World Communications, Sea Sunday,

Racial Justice Sunday, Harvest Festival, Mission Sunday, Prisoners' Sunday, Youth Sunday, and the ninefold Brusselmans communion course. Somehow these have to be integrated with the natural sequence of seasons and holy days, without doing violence to the shape of the liturgical year. I think the diocesan priest suffers the strain of this more than anyone else. It is as if we were being asked to enthuse, to order, fourteen times or more in the year, and to say to our people, 'Now this really *is* important', while not losing sight of the fact that the Mass itself is *always* important, and life-giving beyond words. It isn't that we mind taking the inevitable second collection – as a rule that's no problem, and we understand the need for it. It is that, having been told how basic to Christian existence the liturgy is, and how the homily is part of that exquisite work of art, the Mass in the Roman Rite, we are suddenly showered with extraneous matter, and asked to 'work it in somehow', or to make an exception this week and short-circuit the Scripture, or even short-circuit all the texts of the Sunday's Mass, in favour of something else.

Here is an example of liturgical distraction. I am writing this chapter on a Sunday evening, when the whole nation is mourning the massacre of sixteen primary school children by a deranged gunman in Scotland. The Prime Minister asked for a minute's silence all over the country today, and we incorporated this into the Bidding Prayers. It is also Mothering Sunday, which brings out the daffodils. There was a dilemma today: whether the daffodils should be given by the children to their mothers (at the sign of peace?) or in some symbolic way to the slaughtered children (at the offertory?). This was one of the Sundays, too, when our youngsters disappear into the presbytery for their own Liturgy of the Word, and there is a precise moment for sending them off, just before the Confiteor. If I forget, and leave it any later, the time is so short that it's hardly worth their going. (My catechists have learned to tic-tac to me from the body of the church, like bookies, just to make sure.) It is also St Patrick's Day, which many folk feel should be celebrated with more than a pass-ing nod, especially in view of the fragile situation in Ulster. It is also a staging-point in the R.C.I.A. – the scrutinies, if you're doing things properly; certainly, the Gospel of the man born blind and an application of this to the parish's catechumens. All these elements had their supporters today, pressure groups of one or more, who would nip confidentially into the sacristy as I was vesting for Mass and say, 'You haven't forgotten . . .?' In addition, I have to confess to adding some distraction of my own, because the end of the tax year is approaching, and this is the time when parish priests stir uneasily in their setts like badgers in the spring, and want to make sure people have paid up their covenants and are using the proper envelopes; so I had scheduled, today, a 'State of the Union' message to the whole parish. Finally, the Mass had been earmarked by a parishioner: would I offer it for his grandmother, whose anniversary it was, and, of course, mention her at some point in the proceedings?

I sometimes complain about finding the liturgy uphill work, and an increasing strain, and wonder if this is a sign of age. But I suspect that the things which are such a strain are not the liturgy at all. Maybe one day a new Council will take an axe to the bits and pieces, just as the last one did to the Prayers for the Conversion of Russia and the Last Gospel.

The liturgy includes, obviously, the Prayer of the Church. It is a pity when priests stop saying the Office. I don't mean occasionally, but as a deliberate policy. 'It doesn't help me. It doesn't mean anything to me.' It is a pity because this is, whether they realise it or not, a declaration of individualism. In fact I don't pray in order to be helped, or so that the prayer will mean something to me. If it does, that's a bonus. I pray, however, so that God may be praised by his creation which includes me. I pray so that the voice of the Church may be as ample as it's meant to be. There is a solidarity in this, a solidarity with priests and religious around the world, with mountain friaries and metropolitan cathedrals, with lay communities and contemplative cloisters. It is like taking hold of a rope, and sensing as you do that many others also have their hands on the rope, and are going to pull with you.

Moreover, St John of the Cross would say that it is precisely in the darkest moments, when there is least satisfaction, that we begin to know God. We know him not with creamy emotions or flashes of intuition, but with a sixth sense which cannot be described. An obedient setting-aside of the time, however dry an experience the Prayer of the Church may be, gives space for that sixth sense to operate.

At various times and in various places, I have lived with priests who were good liturgists. They actually 'felt' with the season, being in a Lenten mood in Lent and an Advent mood in Advent. I have never been able to do this. The strain of delivering a correct package to the people in church has, I think, dulled my personal sensibilities. I have always admired men who prepared the Mass minutely, finding the precise preface to echo the Gospel or the homily, the exact introduction to the Our Father. For them, the liturgy was a garden of delights; for me, a bit of a minefield.

But, in another way, the liturgy means a lot to me. I always remember reading, years ago, how the rich burghers of the Athenian Republic, who would have much preferred going to the theatre and discussing philosophy in the market-place, were each told to raise the money for a warship. The Persians were perpetually on the verge of invading Greece. Anyone with a few pence to spare had to do his 'liturgy', his public service, and commission a trireme. What's more, his 'liturgy' included putting to sea as the captain of the ship, and fighting. Prosperity brought its own hazards. Public service meant pulling together all your resources, for the public good.

Our liturgy shares the same character. I am privileged to know the theology of the Church's public prayer, and to have been equipped by ordination to make sure it happens. This makes me, in my own way, a worthy burgher. When I 'do' the liturgy, whether at the altar or through the psalms of the Church's prayer, I am drawing together all the aspirations, sighs, groans, hopes, thankfulness, excitement, resignation, patience of a world which cannot find the language to express them to God. In their name I do the expressing. I am their spokesman, their ambassador. This is my public service, which at times I enjoy very much and at times I enjoy not at all. It's irrelevant, so long as the job is done.

CHAPTER 3

Scandalising the reasonable

I am presuming to add to all the words which have already been written about celibacy. I reflect: here I am, unmarried and unattached at the age of 62. Quite honestly, what has it all been about? I ought to be a grandfather, coasting into retirement with my wife, looking forward to visits from my children and grandchildren, getting in those flights to New Zealand and those cruises round the Norwegian Fjords which active and healthy retirers enjoy so much. Instead, I am still working as a priest, and am viewed by my diocese as having another thirteen active years to offer. Did I get it all monumentally wrong? Isn't it the normal thing for a man to get married, and to retire at an agreed point to enjoy his family to the full, and has anyone, Catholic Church included, got any right to inflict such a wound on my normality? I only have one life, and it is almost over. Have I missed the boat? And if so, whose fault is it?

What I have written here is very western: negative, querulous, doubting, prescinding from the place of the Holy Spirit in my life and the Church's life. But these are the questions that almost ask themselves in our society, because our society doesn't begin to understand celibacy. On the contrary, it greets the whole concept with snorts of derision. As a result, priests don't just have to live it, they also have to defend it. Not only to others, but to themselves.

Is celibacy the last bastion of a humanity-hating, fun-forbidding obscurantism? If so, it's indefensible. Much of the western world thinks it is just that. Simply part of the Catholic Church's dotty attitude to sex, they say. Now, we priests are children of this western culture, and consciously or subconsciously we share most of its assumptions. Do we share this one?

A sketch of the diocesan priest's spirituality has got to take into account his vocation to celibacy. It is a vocation. When the Church calls us forward for ordination, she calls us forward for this too. A positive thing. Not just a 'thou-shalt-not.' Not grim, resentful bachelorhood with lots of built-in compensations. A positive, deliberately chosen way of living the Gospel: this is what we are challenged to. A way which is, astonishingly, fertile.

I remember when I did a foundation course for counsellors, years ago, our tutor introduced us to a book called *Childhood and Society* by Erikson. It is a book which unconsciously mimics Shakespeare's *Seven Ages of Man*, except that it goes one better and gives us eight. Erikson describes the normal developing and maturing process from the cradle to the grave. He shows the tasks to be accomplished at each stage.

The infant must learn to trust; then achieve a degree of autonomy. The primary school child has to learn to focus on goals, plan, undertake; and also to make things work, to use tools. The teenager has to discover who he or she is, amid the upheavals of adolescence. In our twenties we find out not just who we are but *whose* we are: who loves us, defining ourselves by intimacy with partner, friends, family. And in middle years we become generative – not just by having babies, which will already have happened if it's going to happen, but by passing on our wisdom, sharing our experience of life, enriching the generations which come after us. Finally, there is a period when we gather together the experiences and the memories, and weld them into a whole life, and find it possible to live serenely at peace with that whole life, without undue regret or anxiety.

This is normality. 'Who's normal?' you may ask, which is a good question. We may not accomplish each stage at the copy-book age. Some of us are slow developers. But for a happy, contented and fulfilled life, this is the way we shall have to travel. Married or single, this is our path. The question is: can those crucial mid-stages of intimacy and generativity be accomplished by someone who is celibate? Or can they only mean genital intimacy, physical generativity?

I believe that – because, and only because the Spirit is in the mix – celibate priests can enjoy intimacy with God, and with other men and women, and that this intimacy is authentic and real. And I have known so many men, and women (celibacy not being the preserve of priests, or of religious people at all) who from the strongpoint of their celibacy have enriched the lives of whole generations, and have filled for them a truly grandparental role. It is the kind of paradox you find in Isaiah (49:18-21):

Look round about you, look,
all are assembling, coming to you,
By my life – it is Yahweh who speaks –
you will wear these as your jewels,
they will adorn you as brides are adorned;
for your desolate places and your ruins
and your devastated country
will now be too small for all your inhabitants,
now that your devourers are far away.
Once more they will speak in your hearing,
those children you thought were lost,
'This place is too small for me,
give me more space to live in.'
You will then say in your heart,
'Who has borne me these?
I was childless and barren,
who has bought these up?
I was left all alone,
and now, where do these come from?'

The spiritual children I have generated by school visits, by R.C.I.A. evenings, by Sunday homilies, by kind words at the moment of Reconciliation, by marriage preparation, and at night calls to the hospital, all these will be revealed to me, jostling for position they'll be, around the Father's table in the kingdom, trying to catch my eye and saying, 'Do you remember when . . . ?' and 'I shall never forget what you said

. . .' And I, who thought in my blackest moments that celibacy had devastated my life, making me a bizarre and irrelevant curiosity, mournful like the owl on the roof in Psalm 102, and that God must view me as a desolate place and a ruin, will discover with tears of relief and gratitude that I was, after all, supremely fertile, and fruitful in ways I'd never dreamt possible, fruitful in ways which will register all through eternity. The 'devourers' in my life were not celibacy, but cynicism and depression. Hannah, in 1 Samuel 2, sings her song of thankfulness and exultation, the barren woman who bears sevenfold because 'there is none as holy as Yahweh, no rock like our God'. This song will be ours.

In the meantime, the living of celibacy can be tough. How to make spiritual sense of the experience? It seems to me that the only way is in terms of the Crucifixion. What Christ did for me was over the top. What he endured out of love was excessive, prodigal, generous to a fault and beyond a fault. The Way of the Cross is like an object lesson hammered home again and again: 'I love you, I love you, can't you get it into your head that I love you?' The Crucifixion, quite honestly, doesn't make sense. It doesn't make sense that Our Lord should undergo all that psychological and physical misery, that whole black pit of suffering, for take-it-or-leave-it Christians like me. Somehow, the proportions seem wrong. I honestly don't merit that intensity of salvation. Calvary, in that sense, is crazy. Paul has it, doesn't he, in Romans (5:7): 'It is not easy to die even for a good man – though of course for somebody really worthy, a man might be prepared to die – but what proves that God loves us is that Christ died for us while we were still sinners.' If Jesus, my brother, went that far down the line for me, my love for him needs to bear that same stamp of – dare I say it? – unreasonableness. Like the woman who poured the costly nard over his feet, scandalising the reasonable Judas, I need to expend for him the most precious thing I have. Celibacy is the nearest thing I can manage to a response in kind. After my desire to live, my sexuality is the most deeply rooted element in me. And celibacy has the value of being, not a once-and-for-all sacrifice, but a daily one, which is fair, for I reap daily the benefits of his Passion and Death.

Our sexuality is more basic to our whole way of being than we realise. We were sexual men and women even in the womb, and in our infancy: pleasures of touch and feeling were part of our development long before we had the power to reflect on them. When we were foetuses, our reproductive system evolved in the same central layer of cells as our blood-circulation. Sexuality is as much part of us as our heartbeat. As little children, we became aware of our genitality long before it occurred to us that it carried a moral implication. Genital activity isn't a thing apart, an on/off function which can be controlled as though by a switch; it is a continuum with the whole sensual side of us, and the sensual side is as much God's creation as the intellectual and the spiritual. All our relationships are filtered through our sexuality, are the product of our sexual selves. This isn't fanciful talk. I can no more unsex myself than I can disembody myself.

So celibacy, too, is a way of being sexual. I have a God-given power to be intimate, to be affectionate, to draw people to myself and to respond, too, to their signals of attraction, to charm and be charmed. This power is integral to my humanity. If I try to excise it I shall do myself irreparable damage. Celibacy isn't an excision, but a canalisation. It is a decision to symbolise, in our own lives, the universality of God's love for people.

Some people are unfortunate enough to be tone-deaf. If you play them a symphony, they may listen politely, but they won't hear what you hear. Some people are unfortunate enough to be colour-blind. Show them the 'Last Judgement' in the Sistine Chapel, and they can see the shape of the thing, and its composition, but the vividness is lost on them. Some people have very literal, mechanical minds: readings from Gerard Manley Hopkins only annoy them. Some Christians find the sacramental theology of Catholics quite incomprehensible, because it calls on notions of symbol and analogy which are foreign to them. In other words, all of us have blind spots.

Some people – quite a lot of people – find the idea of celibacy for the sake of the kingdom simply ridiculous. They will point, with justice, to the holy and productive lives of thousands of Christian ministers who are married. They will rehearse the famous arguments about only married people understanding the problems of married people. They will produce various proofs that the presbyters of apostolic and sub-apostolic times were married. They will hint darkly (and unfairly) that celibacy is the seedbed for child-abuse. They will claim, possibly rightly, that if some priests were allowed to marry, South America would produce its own vocations and the extreme Protestant sects wouldn't have the walkover they do. The will reflect, rightly again, that celibacy has often been the main component in the creation of a clerical caste which is ambitious, powerful and far too exclusive, reducing the laity to a purely passive and paying role. But in dismissing celibacy as a way of living the Gospel, they betray a blind spot.

The Church sturdily maintains the value of the celibacy of hundreds of thousands of her ministers, and of her sons and daughters in religious life. At our baptism, Paul tells us, we 'put on Christ'. During our lives we try, clumsily enough, to make this really come true, to conform ourselves to Christ. Part of this conforming process, for some of us Christians at least, is our chosen single state: we become as much like the Lord as we can. It isn't an implied criticism of those who marry. It isn't an assertion of superiority. There isn't, lurking in our celibacy, an ambiguous attitude to human sexuality. We're not saying, 'Everyone should be like us.' We're simply saying, 'For me, because of the vocation I have and the gift the Lord has given me, celibacy is right. I don't perceive it as an all-negative prohibition. I see it as a way through, in love, to the Lord who is the centre of my life. And also to an awful lot of people. Not a denial of relationship, but a power and a freedom to relate, and to love.'

CHAPTER 4

Collaborative ministry

Do you remember the theologian called Avery Dulles, who became famous for his 'models of the Church'? He was really saying this: there are various ways of thinking of the Catholic Church. You can think of it as an Institution, with a chain of command inside it. You can think of it as the Body of Christ, where all are equal in the sight of God although they have different, and interconnecting vocations. You can think of the Church as a Herald of the word of God, the world's prophetic conscience, recalling it powerfully to its duty to God. You can think of the Church as Servant, coming to the practical aid of suffering humanity. You can think of the Church as the Praying Heart of the human race, adoring God in the name of those who do not yet know him. You can think of the Church as Witness – witness to the justice of God. (Not all these models are Dulles'; some of them are mine.) I have a friend who is a Pakistani theologian, and he says the most important models are the Ladder (involving superiors and inferiors, jealousy, climbing, and a lot of loneliness) and the Dancing Circle (joyful, shared, with always room for one more). And so on.

The thing about models is that they aren't mutually exclusive. You don't have to say, 'If the Church is this, then it can't be that.' In a way, the exercise is about the thinker. If this is how I primarily see the Church, what kind of person am I? If I think of it mainly as a disciplinary body, what does that say about me? If I see the Church mainly as a rescuer of the poor, does this indicate that I underestimate the need to live a spiritual life? Not necessarily, but the question is still worth asking. If the idea of the Church as a stern denouncer of injustice doesn't interest me, where *do* I stand with regard to oppressed people? Am I so much a liturgical and doctrinal animal that my social awareness is dulled? Models of the Church lead to self-discovery.

We live the models, without realising it. Some of us live outside the sacramental unity of the Church – because of problems of lifestyle, as they say – but still powerfully support its Third World programme, and count ourselves very much as Catholics. Or we can be very precise about the moral law, with the tenderest of consciences, but utterly blank when it comes to ecumenism. We can be great movers and stirrers over the anti-abortion campaign, but conspicuously absent at Justice and Peace events. We declare our model by the way we are.

Now one model which is strongly present in our parishes is the Clerical one. According to this the Church is, for all practical purposes, the Clergy. Other people are admitted to it in a subordinate capacity by being baptised. But 'The Church' means the Pope, the bishop, the priest and deacons, in other words the Uniformed Branch. (Most of the clergy are paid for what they do, and most of them are full-timers. These elements are, after all, the ways our world has of identifying where true responsibility lies.) Similarly, 'vocation' means, for all practical purposes, a call to be a priest or religious. We give lip-service to the vocation of husband and wife, mother and father, teacher and doctor, trade unionist and poet. But when the Bishop says to us, 'Preach about vocations,' we are pretty sure that he wants candidates for the seminary, and no messing. He, like us, works out of the clerical model.

Many priests subscribe to this model without realising it. I suspect I do myself, though in an argument I would hotly deny it. Old habits (of thought) die hard. My train of reasoning would be, 'If I am not considered fit to call the shots in the domain of parish life, then where is my area of competence? If everybody can shape the liturgy, and arrange second collections, and explain the Gospel, without reference to the traditions or norms of Catholicism, what am I here for?' Grinding of teeth, followed by identity crisis. Priests are fragile. I had a difference of opinion with a catechist who was using what I considered inappropriate material for the children's liturgy. When sweet persuasion and all my diplomatic wiles had failed, I fired what I saw as the clinching shot: 'Ultimately, I think you have to leave it to the priest to decide – that's what he's trained for, and that's what the Bishop sent him here to do,' and she replied, quite unclinched, 'Oh no, Father, in this parish we are all equal and we all do our bit as best we can.' Why did I feel so angry?

Many layfolk, unlike my catechist, share the clerical model. Composers of bidding prayers betray their pattern of thought when they write, 'Let us pray for the Church, for Our Holy Father John Paul, for the Cardinal, for our Bishop, for Fathers Jack and Jim, and for priests and missionaries everywhere. Lord, hear us.' Sometimes they show what they really think when they say, 'Father, there's water coming through the roof of your church, and I think you ought to get it fixed.' *My* church? I can't blame them. They've caught it off me.

It is not surprising that when Parish Councils were introduced, the first question asked by many priests was, 'Are they legislative, or merely consultative?' In other words, 'Who's in charge here?' A legitimate question, but a hierarchical one, indicating the model out of which the speaker was working. When people gather in charity, with the highest of motives, is the distribution of power within the group the first thing that needs to be settled? Or would it be better to see what new energy has been harnessed for the furtherance of the Gospel, what new prospects are opening up to make the Church more obviously the Body of Christ? It all depends, as they say, on where you're coming from.

I must confess that I'm not very good at Parish Councils, and they tend to wither, not because I close them down or do them violence, but because, in the same way that I neglect house-plants, I don't feed them enough. They shouldn't need feeding, I know; they should be allowed to nourish themselves, but it doesn't always work. At the beginning I try to say, 'Lift up your eyes to the mountains from which your salvation comes,' and steer them into making the parish a powerful, if potential, evangeliser. When they reply, 'That airy-fairy stuff is all very well, but if we don't get a reliable window-cleaner we shall be in trouble,' I lose heart. I should be more persistent, I know, and return to the attack. If the clergy in the past have taught the laity that their job was to 'help Father' by being hewers of wood and drawers of water, I should put at least as much effort into teaching them that they have a right to share in the policy-making and the spiritual quality of the parish. The people in the parish are quite capable of discerning spiritual and social priorities, but for so many centuries they haven't had the language in which to do it, and they haven't had the chance to grow the muscles.

A spirit of partnership is so different from an atmosphere of domination. Partnership has a powerful theological base: domination does not. The theological base for partnership is the Trinity. God is, so to speak, company: he is sharing, and conversation, and interaction, Father, Son and Holy Spirit; and this is his profound way of being. If I am made in his image and likeness, this urge and need to co-operate and to share must be in me too: it is the proper human way to proceed. It gets overlaid with lonely power and authority only because we are afraid, and need to defend ourselves against being annihilated, or humiliated, or taken for granted. A spirit of partnership does not conflict, even, with the correctly under-stood hierarchical nature of the Church. In the Church the point of structure is to make partnership work, to facilitate it, grease the machine, oil the wheels, not supplant partnership and reduce people to passivity. In other words, hierarchy is at the service of communion. Hierarchy, properly exercised and lived, makes real what Jesus said to the ten Apostles, angry at the jockeying for position of the sons of Zebedee, in Mark 10:41: 'You know that among the pagans their so-called rulers lord it over them, and their great men make their authority felt. This is not to happen among you. No; anyone who wants to become great among you must be your servant, and anyone who wants to be first among you must be slave to all. For the Son of Man himself did not come to be served but to serve, and to give his life as a ransom for many.'

One thing has become clear to me. Whenever you decide to take the laypeople of your parish into your confidence and into real partnership, it's the women who shine. Their willingness to devote time and ingenuity to the most difficult tasks has been an eye-opener to this priest, who has come up through a narrow, male corridor of public school and seminary. Some of the best Chairs of School Governors, with the most accurate instinct for what should and shouldn't be, are mothers of children at the school. Some of the best organisers and marshallers of readers and eucharistic ministers are women. The ones who turn up to perfect their ministry, whatever it is, when some in-service training is offered, are women. The most dogged and persevering co-ordinators of parish councils are women. It is often one of the sisters in the local convent who is the best and wisest spiritual director in the parish, although she might not dignify it with this title. When you come across a priest who is congenitally irritated by women, or dismissive of them, or sees them as no more than flower-arrangers and porch-brushers, you have to do with a handicapped man.

It is a shame that the highlighting of collaborative ministry has coincided with a (comparative) shortage of clergy. The impression is given that if there aren't sufficient priests around to do everything, we should make do with second best and delegate some jobs to laypeople. I would want to fight this impression with all my strength, because I believe it to be totally false. The myth of the omnipotent cleric stems not from the power of Holy Orders, but from the fact that in centuries past the priest was often the only literate person in a community. This is so clearly not the case today that it is laughable for us priests to arrogate to ourselves all the organising capabilities and strategic planning, all the articulation of faith in a parish, all the financial duties.

I believe the future of the Catholic Church in England and Wales lies along these lines, the lines of collaborative ministry. A recent publication (1995) of our Bishops, *The Sign We Give*, deserves re-reading and internalising. It contains accurate and simple statements. And one of them is this:

> When men and women collaborate in ministry, they cannot avoid entering the complex territory of understanding the complementarity of masculine and feminine within and between persons. Indeed, the Trinitarian basis of collaboration demands openness in this aspect of relationships. It may be highly charged and may seem risky to some, but it is one of the ways in which collaborative ministry offers a possibility of profound personal and spiritual growth.

Profound personal and spiritual growth. My blossoming as a son of God, ripe for heaven, doesn't happen apart from my partnership with parishioners, men *and* women, or in spite of it. It happens by means of it.

CHAPTER 5

Desert

Diocesan priests are not like members of religious orders. We have no holy Founder and no holy Rule. We need to construct our own ways of trying to live the Gospel authentically. Our job is to foster the spiritual lives of our parishioners, but in order to do this we need ourselves to have a real relationship with God, something substantial and firm. It is desperately hard to do this in a busy parish, where so many things happen suddenly, and there is little that could be described as 'regular'. We need help: it is almost impossible to be disciplined and ordered in your spiritual life if you are going it alone.

For sixteen years now, I have belonged to something called 'Jesus Caritas'. It's a voluntary association for secular priests, and it was founded in France in 1951. It is loosely modelled on the writings and example of Charles de Foucauld, and inspired by the life of the Little Brothers and Little Sisters of Jesus. There are little Jesus Caritas groups all over the world. You could say they are mutual support groups, and that is true. But in fact they are something extra. Jesus Caritas is more than a series of shoulders to lean on, vital though this is. It tries to be a way of taking the Gospel seriously, and to provide an across-the-board spirituality which suits the precise situation of the diocesan priest. For six years I was the 'International Responsible' of Jesus Caritas, which made me a professional traveller and visitor. I came into contact with many hundreds of diocesan priests in all five continents. What I experienced both humbled and inspired me.

Alvaro Gonzalez had been elected, with a third priest (the parish priest of Harlem in New York), to form with me the international team of Jesus Caritas. He was a Chilean priest who worked with university students. He was chaplain to 80,000 of them, a number which made me blink with disbelief when first he told me. He was also a psychologist, and he spent his afternoons piecing together broken marriages in the slum-suburbs of Santiago. Well, in 1989 I went with Alvaro to Indonesia, to spend a month with some Asian priests. It was a special kind of month, what we call the Month of Nazareth, the nearest thing Jesus Caritas has to a thirty-day retreat. It was the first time it had happened in Asia. It was to be an exercise in simple, lowly community living.

So we flew to Jakarta in an air-conditioned, cushioned Lufthansa jet, and emerged into a blaring, sticky porridge of a city. The traffic pollution was incredible. The river, beneath the bridges, was fringed with great settlements of precarious houses, and covered with scum. The noise was deafening – querulous pings and squawks from the bells and horns of bicycle-taxis, full-throated bellows from the lorries, muezzins shouting from the tops of mosques, crowds of people chattering in the street-markets.

Here we met the other men with whom we would be spending the month, all diocesan priests. Two from Pakistan, one from Taiwan, two from Bangladesh, one from Sri Lanka, a German missionary, three from the Philippines. Together we got on a bus, and travelled for a day and a night east from Jakarta, into the mountains of central Java. The bus puttered along the hill roads, and the driver played silky Javanese music, inconsequential pipe-trilling music which wound itself into my brain, and the breeze blew the curtains into my face, and I wondered intermittently, between naps, how the hell I had got to this point in my life with this extraordinary crowd of people, and what exactly did I think I was doing, and had I honestly anything to offer them? I also reflected that the Catholic priesthood is an extraordinary thing. Here I was with eleven men whose upbringing and outlook were so different from my own. Yet there was so much we held in common that we hardly had to mention it. There was so much we could take for granted about one another.

The Sri Lankan was a Tamil, a teacher with a degree in English literature from an American university. His country was in the middle of a civil war. At home, he would sit under a tree with his students and they would placidly discuss the meaning of life; he would then set out by bicycle for the college where he taught, often dodging shells and bombs, to be in time for seminars and lectures. In the evening he would visit his parishioners, and comfort those whose husbands, brothers and sons had been found dead in ditches. It was a grotesque sequence of tranquillity and violence, but it had been going on for so long that he was used to it. He had the true versatility of the diocesan. The Taiwanese ran, single-handed, the Young Christian Workers in Taipei. The German had lived for fifteen years in Dhaka, and had developed a powerful centre there for interfaith dialogue. The Bangladeshis were very young, laughed a lot, and had only been priests for a few weeks. One of the Filipinos was so small and slight that he looked like a boy, but he was running one of the biggest and toughest parishes in Manila. Another lived in the heart of bandit-country in Mindanao. The Pakistanis were leaders of Christian communities in the most abrasively hostile and difficult places, stern, moustachioed, impressive men. Their life was so uncushioned by comparison with mine; they had all known poverty, some of them had experienced real danger and persecution, some had been grossly overworked and had learned to pace themselves . . . they were wise men. What had placid, middle-class parochial Britain to say to them? What did they care about Apostolicae Curae, or the Latin Mass Society, or the latest comprehensive R.E. syllabus, or any of the things which peopled my life at home? Quietly and politely, on the bus, I had a deep crisis of confidence, an inward yell of panic, and began to lose my nerve.

We settled into a Jesuit retreat centre near Semarang. It was very austere by European standards. No shower or bath

– just a vat of water, which you poured over yourself from a saucepan. Plentiful mosquitoes, adept at getting inside the thickest net. Guinea-fowl on the lawn, meandering between exotic bushes with bright red flowers, shrieking and cackling. A chapel built of corrugated iron and plastic, which contracted and expanded in the heat with noises like gunfire. Booby-trapped food, most of which was delicious, but containing in every fifth dish a knock-out dose of chilli. I could not manage the fish with the thousand bones, and watched fascinated as the other men crunched the whole lot up with blissful expressions. Nor could I bring myself to eat without a knife and fork. I became painfully conscious of my prejudices and cultural limitations. It was all very good for my pride.

So was the manual work which went with the Month. The Jesuits asked us to plant a forest of papaya trees in their orchard, and this meant digging holes a metre square and a metre deep. The ground was muddy and we had no spades, only mattocks. In the international papaya-planting league, I regret to report that the United Kingdom was unplaced. The Pakistanis excelled in the production of holes. 'I will show you how the Pathans can dig,' said Solomon – who was racially Goanese, not Pathan at all – and there was a sudden hail of clay as he wielded his mattock over his head, attacking the ground like a mastiff, pouring with sweat, deadly accurate, seeming to know by instinct when to stop because the job was done, and there was this neat, square cavity, and there was this cubic metre of dirt, and it had all happened in something under a minute.

Then, on another day, I was sauntering through this village. We had all dispersed at crack of dawn to spend a day alone. The idea was to be alone with God, to spend the day in prayer and reflection, letting God come, so to speak, and find us. It is what the hermits in the desert had done from the time of St Antony. I was searching for a quiet place, away from people, but as the hours passed I came to the gradual realisation that the middle of Java is populated in every corner without exception; even the jungle is full of houses. Mine was a very self-conscious saunter, because I was aware of being at least a foot taller than everyone else within sight, and infinitely fatter and pinker. It was getting on for midday, and the heat was massive; I glistened as I walked. I had dressed for the day in what I had fondly imagined to be inconspicuous clothes, a pair of slacks and a nondescript sports shirt, with a baseball cap perched on top of my white hair to keep the sun off my head, and a small haversack for a sandwich and a bottle of water. The result was, to the Javanese, astonishing and uproarious. Had I arrived in a flying saucer, stark naked and with green ears, I could not have caused more of a sensation.

As I passed the village primary school, the lessons stopped, the door burst open, and all the children tumbled out on to the road to gape. I pretended not to notice and continued doggedly sauntering. They followed, their knuckles pressed into their mouths with excitement. When I stopped and turned, they stopped; it was like a game of Grandmother's Footsteps. I never discovered what happened to their teacher, or got a chance to apologise for what had happened to her class. We got to the end of the built-up part of the village, and they were still there, twittering in the dust twenty yards behind me. We passed a couple of paddy fields and went through a belt of palms and bananas, with the small houses dotted about among the trees – their family houses, I supposed. At each moment I expected their enraged fathers to appear, brandishing sharp instruments and accusing me of kidnapping: the scene was becoming more and more reminiscent of the Pied Piper. I stopped and searched desperately for the small Indonesian dictionary in my pocket. Looking severe, I extended my finger back along the road. 'To school!' I thundered sternly. At this they fell about in the sun, tears of delight streaming down their cheeks, and imitated to one another what I had just said.

Eventually I lost them by walking down a steep slope to a river. The only bridge over the river was a wide plank; there were no handrails, I noticed. I turned, and there were no children either, they had vanished. Maybe the bridge was bad news for the youngsters in the village, maybe some of them had fallen off in the past, and so their parents had declared it off-limits? I walked gingerly across and on, trying to collect my thoughts and refocus on the Lord who had led me into the desert in order to seduce me, but had instead organised this unaccountable and lengthy distraction. I was saying to him, 'I really did try – if this desert day is a washout, Lord, it is your fault.' And he replied, 'You have a very narrow and conventional idea of what the desert is all about; you forget that the desert is populated, and that I know and love the people in it, and that you can find my face in theirs.'

There were other such days which were quieter. On one of them I sat on a hillside among the trees, and watched the lorries and water-buffalo-carts far off in the valley. The sun moved over me – directly over – and I kept shifting under the trees to find the shade. I had a moment of intuition that in fact the earth was revolving under the sun, and that I was being revolved on it, rolled under the sun, and that God was as inevitable and as present as a Javanese sun; that I was Man under God, that was my basic identity and status, and nothing could really mask me from him, and life was simply a matter of being revolved under God. The red ants began to take a serious interest in my extremities, and the call to prayer began from half a dozen mosques in nearby villages. There was a shrill, imperious one about five miles off in the forest; a much more laid-back, throaty one at the foot of my hill; a late starter over to the left. They called me to prayer, too, even if I was clutching my New Testament and musing on Colossians: 'He is the image of the unseen God, and the first-born of all creation . . . before anything was created, he existed, and he holds all things in unity.' The voice from the stubby minaret would not have given Christ this cosmic importance. But, then, perhaps he wasn't really a voice but just a tape in a cassette player. I shall never know.

These quiet days are a strange experience, but so very, very valuable. They bring you face to face with yourself, with your need of props and resources, and your smallness without them. They are a way of confronting your own poverty, and this throws you on to God in a new way. It is afterwards, when you reflect on the experience, that you realise how valuable it was; a glimpse of the truth like the glimpse of a peak by mountaineers for whom the mist momentarily clears. I begin to see why Charles de Foucauld had found the Sahara so attractive. He was only allowed to move about the desert with military contingents, but even so he managed to guard his silence and his recollection. Pierre Mille, one of the young soldiers who marched with him in the 'Colonne Dinaux' from Beni-Abbès to Tamanrasset, said, 'We used to laugh at his extraordinary passion for the desert. We were an insensitive bunch of youngsters, and we used to refer to him, among ourselves, as the guy who always felt that the trams were too close.'

In fact the desert is not an escape from the trams. It equips us to confront reality, and have relationships which are honest, and deep. Henri Nouwens, in his book *Reaching Out*, distinguishes loneliness from solitude. Loneliness makes you a leech, makes you dependent on people, demanding. Solitude means you are content with your own company, balanced and in the best sense self-sufficient; which means that working from this firm base – being 'bien dans ta peau' – you can be a friend to a large number of folk without exploiting them. A lot of our spiritual life is spent in making this transition from loneliness to solitude. Charles de Foucauld made this transition. Before his conversion he experienced loneliness, and exorcised it with love affairs which, ultimately, did not satisfy. The first fifteen years after his conversion were a discovery of solitude, an exploration of solitude, saying goodbye to his family, joining the Trappists, going to Nazareth. The second fifteen, which ended with his death, were devoted to poor and forgotten people in Algeria, in a myriad of different ways, not grudgingly like a hermit interrupted in his contemplation, but with great joy, as the principal business of life. There was a doctor who spent time with him, Dr Hérisson, and he used to say that Charles was the opposite of other great men, because the closer you got to him, the greater he got. The desert did not make him unapproachable. The reverse was true.

I had gone to Indonesia expecting to find that the Catholic Church was very small and ineffective, and that the Muslim majority was hostile. I had pictures in my mind of ancient, wrinkled Dutch missionaries in huts in jungle clearings, with tiny congregations. The reality surprised me. First, the Catholic Church is only a tiny percentage of the whole population in Java – perhaps two per cent – but two per cent of all those millions makes a sizeable crowd. Then, the Church has put her energy into institutions, into clinics and hospitals and colleges and schools, which are of very high quality, so that the influential and rich Indonesians want to use them. The difference of faith does not seem to matter at this level, perhaps because the Indonesians sit rather lightly to all religions, and tend to blend them together instead of opposing them. One young priest told me how his mother, although she was a convert to the Catholic Church, would at times of illness still consult the white witch at the end of her village. 'And,' he said pensively, 'it works.' The social status of a Catholic priest in a village in Central Java was astonishingly high. The seminary in Semarang was full, and the diocese was sponsoring many thousands of catechumens. The spectre of Muslim fanaticism was not immediate, because the military government would not let it get the upper hand; a degree of religious tolerance was built into the Constitution. The downside of this arrangement was, of course, that the Church had an interest in the continuation of the military government, which, however, was dictatorial and which had at times been terribly ruthless in crushing opposition. The story of East Timor is an illustration of this. Paradoxes . . . some of the old

Dutchmen who had been in the former East Indies since before the Second World War, and who had been imprisoned by the Japanese, were still there. These missionaries spoke better Javanese, often, than the Javanese themselves. In order to remain in the country they had taken Indonesian citizenship, which meant that on their infrequent visits to Holland they had to stand in the 'alien' queue at the immigration desk in Amsterdam Airport.

Evidently the Church was developing along highly successful institutional lines; I wondered about the side of faith which is content to be small, contemplative, wondering, ineffective, caught up in mystery – a side I had expected to discover in the East, rather than the western model of efficiency and achievement. Our Sri Lankan told us one evening about the Hindus and the Buddhists at home in Jaffna. He told us what they asked about the Christians. 'We see your big white office blocks for the diocesan administration. We see your jeeps and cars, supplied by the Germans. We see your efficiency. But where are your gurus? Where are your holy men? Whom do you consult for spiritual guidance? You have no one. All you produce is brahmins (administrators).'

Now I'm home in England, eight years on from this trip to Indonesia, and my official travelling days are over. But the dilemma continues to tease and worry me. I can see how vital institutions are. I can see the incredible good done, for example, by our Catholic schools over the years. I can see that without institutions many of our people would be unable to express their identity in any way. I can see that parishes with churches and halls and clubs provide a focus by which people can make their 'belonging' concrete, and have concrete things to be proud of, to defend, to enhance. But I can also see that the maintenance of institutions can become a colossal red herring, and at worst a substitute God, sucking up all our energy and ingenuity. We must leave something over for the naked eyeball-to-eyeball encounter with God, which takes place in tranquillity, sometimes boredom, often darkness.

Unbolstered by committees and development plans, it is only then that I appreciate how small I am, how helpless I am, how much I depend on Almighty God. Only in that kind of prayer do I discover that Christian community is not about pecking-order, power and authority, but about a humble and humorous sharing of how much God has blessed us.

Ultimately, it's nothing to do with Jesus Caritas or Charles de Foucauld. I'm writing this simply as a diocesan priest, for diocesan priests. We are open to interruption and demands on our time, all the time. Impossible to say how often the telephone and the doorbell have called us out of church. We have learned, more or less, to control our temper and our tongue. After all, we pray in order to be better servants of the people; we pray for their sake, not just ours. But sometimes it's hard to retain composure.

Spiritually, a diocesan priest has to be enormously flexible. It is not possible, it seems to me, to stick to a rigid programme of sacrosanct times for prayer without becoming forbidding pastors, and also without being obsessive and over-severe with ourselves. The prayer which is not done in the morning can be done in the evening, and the supercharged day can be compensated at another time in the week. It is, however, crystal clear that we need not only to pray, but from time to time to take ourselves off into the desert, so that God can speak to our heart. The busier we are, the more this matters. The diocesan priest, more than anyone else in the Church's range of ministers, is planted in the world, in the middle of it and not on the fringe of it. He needs therefore to be a man who sees the world around him with a contemplative eye, relating it all the time in his thoughts to God, to the will and the heart and the glory of God. Where do you go for a contemplative eye? To the desert. To those times when you are alone, like the times spent by Jesus on the bare mountain when the disciples were asleep. Into our flexibility we must build solitude.

CHAPTER 6

Uncharted territory

It is terrible to be on the sidelines when a friend loses his bearings. A few years ago I went to a meeting in the south of Belgium, the French-speaking part, and was due to catch a train at the end of it. Philippe, a priest I had known for years, said he would run me to the station. We were early, so we made for the bar, and a pint.

It was the pint which unleashed the torrent. As he drank he began to talk. He had been ordained a priest in 1968. 'At that time,' he said, 'I was somebody in the village. I had status. Even people who did not practise their religion were civil and polite, they greeted me in the street, they recognised me. Now, in my parish, they just look through me. I am the invisible man. It is as though I do not exist.' The early-evening crowds hurried past us, unwittingly illustrating his point. Belgium had moved with rapidity from a genial, clerical, tribal religion with custom and folklore built into it, to a secular society revolving round the supermarket. No staging-posts. At one moment, collective faith – making, admittedly, no great demands on the individual, except that he should go to Mass from time to time and refrain from voting Socialist – the next, gross consumerism and a wholesale desertion of the Church, even by the children of the most pious parents. In 1831 when Belgium was invented by the Great Powers, its *raison d'être* had been that the people were Catholics. An ironic reflection.

Philippe, like most French and French-speaking priests, had been trained in the methods of Catholic Action. He was accustomed to see society in horizontal layers. He was conscious of the social class of everyone he met, and of his own.

He came from a poor industrial family, and was most at home with the families of coalminers and steelworkers. However, in the '80s and '90s, in Belgium as in England, the coalmines had been closed and the steel factories eliminated. His whole ideology, like that of the Y.C.W. in England, had been this: the Christian must penetrate the milieu of industry, and make the Gospel, with its accent on integrity and justice, come true for the working classes. Suddenly, in mid-life, he had no milieu to penetrate. How do you penetrate the milieu of the unemployed?

'And what is more,' he said bitterly, 'we now have a bishop who thinks the way to reconvert our country is to stage Pontifical Vespers in the Cathedral, and dress all his Canons up in vestments.' He glared into his glass reproachfully, as if the guilty prelate were somewhere at the bottom of it. I did not know how to console him. He felt that he had been cheated, cheated of the only envelope into which he personally could fit his Christianity and his priesthood. He was like Rachel in the prophecy of Jeremiah, weeping for her children and refusing to be comforted, because they were no more.

My train arrived. As it pulled away I looked back out of the window and he was there on the platform, gaunt and somehow marooned beneath a lamp, staring after me in a bewildered way through his horn-rimmed spectacles, swathed to the chin in a thick scarf, affronted and hurt under his beret. It was the last time I saw him.

In England we, too, have coped more or less well with a tidal wave of materialism. We too feel bewildered at the sheer intensity of irreligion on the housing estates and in the tower blocks. It isn't just a lazy, casual, laid-back attitude to Church and religious practice. It is not just the lack of something. It is a culture in its own right. It is something positive and virulent. It burns like a flame and is consuming the faith of a whole generation. You are aware of it in the media, where God is mocked. You are aware of it in schools, where R.E. is often well taught, but simply not absorbed, because it is the Cinderella of subjects, and the youngsters have built up a resistance to it. You're aware of it when young couples come to get married, and you try to make sense of religious concepts for them when all they can think of is the siting of the photographer. You're aware of it in the bookshops, where Christianity now has a shelf or two among the 'Paranormal and Esoteric'.

I suppose it is marginally less distressing for us than it is for Philippe, because as Catholics in England we are used to being a minority. Priests, on the whole, cannot say, 'Once I was somebody in the village.' We are accustomed to being largely ignored, not heard. The non-hearing Establishment was once vaguely but officially Christian. Now it is openly derisive of us, of all Christians, and of what we believe in. And Catholicism, with its stand on medical-moral issues, is even more counter-cultural than other denominations. The Gospel is harder to preach and to share than it has ever been. It is hard to get a handle on it: we know what the Gospel is about, we know its truth and its power, but it needs translating, and we cannot find the idiom.

For a diocesan priest this is especially painful. The secular world is our stomping-ground, our natural habitat. We know that the Gospel can transform and heal this world. Our job is to put them in touch with one another. But how?

Not surprisingly, I do not have a complete answer to this. However, here are a few reflections which might provide a beginning.

The first is about compassion. Mark 8:1 *sqq.*: 'In those days when there was again a great crowd without anything to eat, he called his disciples and said to them, "I have compassion for the crowd."' And Matthew 9:36: 'When he saw the crowds, he had compassion for them, because they were harassed and helpless, like sheep without a shepherd.' And Matthew 14:14, where Our Lord has withdrawn in a boat to a deserted place by himself, and the people follow him: 'When he went ashore, he saw a great crowd; and he had compassion for them, and cured their sick.'

It is clear that Jesus saw this crowd of poor and aimless people not as a hostile army ranged against him, but as people deserving compassion. The crowd that surrounds us deserves it no less. If they feel a nervous antagonism in us, they will respond badly. If they experience affection, many good things can happen. The simple fact that we are men of faith, even if sometimes we struggle and wobble, makes us different. The important thing is for us not to lose our nerve, and retreat from the multitude, or to say like the Pharisees in John 7:49: 'This crowd, which does not know the Law – they are accursed.' Our neighbours may have a very approximate moral code, and no discernible faith, but they are still sons and daughters of God, carriers of the divine spark. We must always have a soft spot for them.

It is hard not to say an acid word when the engaged couple in front of you is cheerfully cohabiting, and when the bride-groom-to-be says, 'I don't know if this presents a problem, but I was briefly married once before.' It is hard to be patient when the Chinese restaurant next door spawns half-digested takeaways all over your car park. It is hard to keep your temper when the Council sends a bloke with a pneumatic drill to dig up the road outside the church during the 9.30 Mass on a Sunday morning. It is difficult not to be short when parish-ioners spot you on your day off and make inane remarks about your non-clerical clothes. All these affronts give us an excuse to retire into our mountain fastness with anger, contempt and despair: I have done, and sometimes still do, this.

Or, on the other hand, the occasion can be a springboard for some kind of dialogue, some kind of human contact which *is* human. So long as we don't pull up the drawbridge and let down the portcullis, we shall be available, approachable, and sooner or later they will ask the questions which matter. For the same reason it is good to accept invitations rather than refuse them – to the dreaded wedding reception, where you have to stand on one leg for an hour and a half with people from the bride's firm, while the snapshots are taken; to the buffet after the funeral, where you get cornered by the drunk major with a story to tell; to the county primary school assembly, where the Head is hunting desperately for a speaker ('Next week we've asked the Buddhists'), but where the children are wide-eyed and receptive. None of this is wasted. All of it is compassionate. All of it bears fruit in due time.

The second consideration is this: that what is happening to us, and our world, is happening within Providence, not outside it. God hasn't lost control, any more than he had lost control of the ancient world in which the Apostles worked. Read Romans 8:20: 'For the creation was subjected to futility, not of its own will, but by the will of the one who subjected it, in hope that the creation itself will be set free from its bondage to decay and will obtain the freedom of the glory of the children of God.' Bondage to decay is about right, isn't it? Paul wasn't referring to post-Christian Europe. But the bones of the problem are the same: creation unable to attain its purpose; creation enslaved to decadence; creation groaning in attempts, often misplaced, to attain true freedom.

In a homily at the Missionary Institute in London, the Bishop of Portsmouth said, 'If we are led by the Spirit today – and we believe that we are – then it is not simply to the triumphant and successful proclamation of the Gospel and the consequent liberation of God's world and his people to be what he created them to be. It is also to be led into the wilderness and chaos of a world which has lost its way, a world in which the hand of God is not recognised, and into a human community which seems increasingly dominated by forces which are diabolic.' The point is it's the Spirit who is leading us into – and through – this dark world. We haven't fallen down a manhole of which even the Lord was unaware.

'For in hope we were saved. Now hope that is seen is not hope. For who hopes for what is seen? But if we hope for what we do not see, we wait for it with patience.' (Romans 8:24.) Paul reminds us that we in England are the spiritual heirs of men and women who lived a very long darkness in the most unpromising environment, and never stopped hoping. It is not too much to say that English Catholics are professionals at waiting! It is fascinating to visit little towns in the north of France, like St Omer, and to sense the longing of the English exiles for their faith who lived there in the 16th and 17th centuries: so tantalisingly close to home, and yet destined to die and be buried on the French side of the Channel. There was, indeed, no guarantee that their children or their grandchildren would fare any better. They would go to local schools and be assimilated. Or they would become professional exiles, studying with other groups of expatriates, listening to the rumours of relaxed laws and favourable royal marriages, but always in the end disappointed. They would marry other exiles.

They would acquire the weary endurance that many of us observed, for example, in the Polish people who came to England in 1946. They could not go home because of the Communists. They had never asked to live in England. The English people were kind, and sometimes companionable, and gave them homes and jobs. It was possible to live here in security and with, eventually, a degree of comfort. But the language was wrong. I recall meeting an old lady outside church, one day in 1976, I think it was, when I was trying unsuccessfully to teach myself a little Polish. She fixed me with a beady eye, and said triumphantly 'I have been in this country for thirty-one years and I do not speak a word of English.' She had resisted. To learn English would have meant, mentally, to unpack her bags and put down roots, and this would have been a kind of treachery.

It was not home, but then there was no prospect of going home, and age was creeping on, and the number of Poles in the local cemetery was increasing year by year, and gradually by the 1980s most Polish exiles had settled for the unspeakable, that the frontiers of their homeland were for ever closed, and that here was where you would lay your bones. The fall of the Iron Curtain came too late for tens of thousands of them. 'How can we sing the song of the Lord on alien soil?' We have to make the best of it, and trust in the living Lord to bring all things to their proper conclusion in his own good time.

There is a similar element of exile about our situation. It isn't that we are unhappy in a world of TV and convenience food and dishwashers and the internet. We haven't recoiled from the technological culture, or the comfort and convenience it gives us, quite the reverse. But we know, and preach, that the electronic revolution and the constantly improving chip cannot fulfil the needs of the human soul. To this extent we are oddities, and exiles on our own soil. Yet this is where we have to sing the song of the Lord: there is no other place. And from time to time there is a temptation to surrender, to become like other people, to adopt the language and the values and thought-patterns of the people around us. 'The highland sheep are fleeter, but the lowland sheep are fatter.' If sometimes we abandon the bracing highlands, and mentally settle for the lowlands, I am sure that we must be kind to ourselves, and compassionately understand the reason. We are subjected to the constant strain of being immersed in the Secular City, but not belonging to it. It is as though, to change the metaphor, we had been thrown into a very grim urban canal, and told to swim along it without swallowing any of the polluted water. Not easy. We must love ourselves in our failures, as well as our successes. The Providence of God has made allowances for all this.

I once went to Nairobi. I recall watching the heavy lorries coming up to the highlands from the coast. They drove so slowly through the dried-up countryside – almost at walking pace, you would have said. They were overloaded, and their cargo leaned at crazy angles. From time to time they shed their loads, and the highway was blocked. The vehicles were old, smoky and noisy. They had frequent punctures, and hoisting one of these juggernauts on to a jack to change the wheel was a day's work. The men at the wheel glistened with sweat, and were often caked with the dust thrown up by the truck in front. They had been driving, most probably, for a week or more. In fact, when they settled in behind the wheel, down at Mombasa, and drove in convoy out of the port on to the main road, they knew what they were in for, and mentally paced themselves for hours and days of discomfort and boredom. These were the long-haul men, and the country depended on them.

We too are long-haul men, asked by God to pace ourselves for a lifetime in a faith-desert with not that many oases. We have to pace ourselves, not expect the quick fix or the miracle cure for England's gross materialism, but say an interior 'yes' to the rhythm and routine of driving, slowly but strongly, up a difficult incline. An awful lot of people depend upon us to continue doing this with great patience, and not give up.

The final reflection is this. We are dealing with something entirely new. There is no precedent for a godless world of methodical consumerism. The Catholic Church has been around for twenty centuries, and has fought some monumental battles in that time, sometimes cleanly and sometimes less so. But always the battle has been with people who believed something else. Dealing with a hostile ideology demands certain qualities: character, courage, single-mindedness, clarity of ideas. The resistance of the Church to communism is an illustration of this. So, in a completely different context, is the bravery of the Counter-Reformation martyrs, the razor-sharp responses of men like Bellarmine and Canisius and Campion. Both the Reformers and the Marxists recognised in the Church a formidable adversary, and set about obliterating it as best they could.

Today, the society of Western Europe does not see us as a formidable adversary. Most of the time, it does not see us at all: it sees round us and over us but does not look at us. To be ignored as irrelevant is a new experience for the Church, and it calls for a new set of responses. As St Paul found a new way of preaching for the Athenians, who were a completely new proposition when you compared them with his normal audiences, so must we. Because there is no precedent for this, no one can tell us how to do it. No one has been here before. We must feel free to use our native wit and ingenuity, relying always on the power of God: but not to feel the past weighing on us with reproach. 'Look at Matteo Ricci among the Chinese, and Father Damien among the Polynesian lepers; look at the early missionaries in Sierra Leone, and Bartolome de las Casas in Latin America; why can't you be like them?' We can't be like them, because they were all dealing in some way with people of belief and conviction. We are the first priests to deal with whole populations whose belief-muscles have atrophied, where whole societies have devoted themselves to the knee-jerk pursuit of pleasure. In this sense, I believe, we are pioneers, and we are the ones who have to blaze the trail for those who succeed us. And this, in the historical constellation of the Church's ministers, is a position of great honour: not of shame.

> By faith Abraham obeyed when he was called to set out for a place that he was to receive as an inheritance; and he set out, not knowing where he was going. By faith he stayed for a time in the land he had been promised, as in a foreign land living in tents, as did Isaac and Jacob, who were heirs with him of the same promise. For he looked forward to the city that has foundations, whose architect and builder is God.
>
> (Hebrews 11:8-10)

CHAPTER 7

A noble task

'I'm off,' said my parish priest.

I was astonished. I had only been ordained a few months, and had expected to serve a long apprenticeship with him. He was not an old man. I could not imagine why he wanted to change parishes.

'It's the Bishop,' he said. 'He's asked me twice, you see. Would I like to move, he said. The first time I never answered, so he asked me again. And this is a golden rule which you must learn: if bishops ask you something twice, it's because they want you to do it. So I'm going.'

As an example of intuitive obedience this was second to none. But it fascinated me that this senior priest of the diocese didn't feel sufficiently free to say to the Bishop, 'Can we talk about this? Of course I'll shift if you want me to, but I'd like to know your true feelings about it. Are you doing this for my sake, or for the sake of the parish?' Instead, he treated the Bishop like the Oracle of Delphi, interpreting what he had said, and acting on the interpretation.

This priest, and others of his generation, would be astonished to read, a few years later in *Presbyterorum Ordinis* (7) that the Bishop was to regard his fellow-clergy in the diocese as 'brothers and friends'. Strictly for the birds, they would have said, sheer Vatican-speak. Maybe they didn't want the Bishop as a brother and a friend. Maybe they felt safer with an implacable, olympian authority figure in their lives, whom they would never question, only obey. Much simpler. This would, after all, have been a continuation of their relationship with headmasters, commanding officers, office bosses, seminary rectors; maybe with their own fathers. At that time, it did not seem possible to combine being in charge with real companionship.

It's there again, thirty years later, in *Pastores Dabo Vobis*: 'Just as all can "go" to the Bishop because he is Shepherd and Father to all, his priests who share with him the one priesthood and ministry can do so in a special way: the Bishop, the Council tells us, should treat them as "brothers and friends".'

The link between the Bishop and the diocesan priest is complicated, and it needs exploring. You see, members of religious orders work not under a bishop but an abbot or father provincial, and the abbot or provincial, whether elected or appointed, only serves for a limited time before returning to the ranks. He may be a martinet, but he is not a martinet for ever. The diocesan clergy know, when a bishop is put in place, that – barring promotion – he will be there until he retires, or dies: and that can be a long, long time. So their relationship with him is not just one of liking or disliking, here and now. It's a relationship which has got to work, quite apart from feelings, for ten, twenty years or more. It is a bit like the difference between a republic, where Mr President steps gracefully down, and an absolute monarchy, where Le Roi Soleil holds sway even when the décor of the court begins to peel a bit and the courtiers get rheumaticky and slow. Politicians talk mercilessly about the 'Lame Duck Period' at the end of an administration. An elderly bishop is not necessarily lame, and he is certainly not a duck. Inevitably, though, there will be a contrast between the burst of creative activity in the first years after his installation, and the quiet time when there is illness, or when retirement approaches. Diocesan priests have to live with both, and adapt.

The Bishop has extraordinary authority over a priest's life. He can place him in a small parish, or a large one. He can send him somewhere uncongenial and refuse to move him. He can send him somewhere agreeable and then replace him. There are canonical checks and balances to all this, but they are heavy stuff, and seldom invoked. Quite clearly, clerical appointments are made for the good of the people, not the comfort of the pastors, and a bishop needs the freedom to deploy his men in the best interests of the Church as a whole, and this is a principle we would all accept. However, if a bishop, for good reasons or bad, is critical of a particular priest, and shows it, that priest may have to live in a baleful atmosphere for a good slice of his life. It is true that Canon Law protects the priest's right to look for another diocese and another bishop, but this is a drastic remedy.

A further complication lies in this. Some priests are looking not so much for a brother as for a father. They want the Bishop to be a father-figure in their lives, which means that, while he may chide and nag them, he is ultimately forgiving and indulgent, and will make their burdens his own. It means he will not expect of them high standards of professionalism, in the employer-employee sense. It means that he will be eternally patient with them. If they find they have a bishop who lacks this kind of resigned tenderness, who is an administrator rather than a good listener and sympathiser, who is more formal and less paternal than they had hoped, they are resentful.

The reality may be, and often is, quite otherwise. The Bishop cares for and respects his men, with all their idiosyncrasies and differences, and the respect is reciprocal. He knows instinctively the men he can treat as active co-operators in the business of the diocese, delegating, entrusting and expecting things, and the ones who need more to feel the fatherly umbrella over them. He discusses changes of parish before putting them into effect. There is a real sense of collaboration in the diocese, and real brotherhood and affection both among the priests and between the priests and the Bishop. Students in the seminary sense this, and are glad to belong to this diocese and not another. They are attracted by the humour at diocesan get-togethers, the openness, the ultimate loyalty, and the fact that authority is not exercised arbitrarily, but reasonably.

One of the Canadian bishops at the 1987 Synod said, 'I

have always contended that it takes a lot of good priests to make a bishop look good.' It is tough for a good bishop to find that he cannot treat his men in an adult way. If whatever he says provokes knee-jerk reactions or a neurotic build-up of hurt feelings, he's stuck. If the Council says he must treat his priests as brothers and friends, then they too have to enter into the spirit of the thing. Part of having brothers and friends is that you make allowances for their personal limitations, and that mistakes are allowed, and reconciliation is always possible. Two-way traffic, this.

Bishops are as likely as any other human being to be testy and choleric. Everyone has a right to bad days. If you are off-colour in your family, people take note of it, but they do not hold it against you for ever. Clergy seem to be subject to a different rule. If I speak roughly to a parishioner, there is always the risk that he will go reeling off into the undergrowth and never appear again. In fifty years' time he will be visited in hospital and asked why he has been away from the sacraments for so long. 'Had a row with a priest, Father,' he will reply. Maybe the priest (myself) would have been glad of a chance to apologise, but never got one. The parishioner preferred to play the psychological game of being the Noble Savage, retreating into the bushes and silently licking his wounds. It is a pity if priests play the same game with the Bishop. On the other hand, the Bishop may be as unpredictable and explosive – and dangerous – as Henry VIII. Then it's harder. Priests are sometimes Henry VIII to one another. Years ago, an old parish priest in my diocese was roaring away furiously about something his curate had, or hadn't done. When he had run out of breath the curate, standing in the doorway of his study, said innocently, 'Canon, if I didn't know you better, I'd think you were angry with me.' Collapse of stout party: the point is, though, that the relationship stayed alive.

Ignatius of Antioch on his way to execution in Rome sent letters to the churches of Asia Minor. One of his themes was the need for priests to think with their bishops, and not be rampant individualists. To the Trallians: 'It is the duty of everyone, and most particularly of the clergy, to see that the bishop enjoys peace of mind'; and to the Ephesians: 'Your justly famous presbytery, worthy of God, is attuned to the Bishop as the strings to a harp.' Was *not* being attuned a problem at the start of the second century, or just in the last quarter of the twentieth? I suspect that in the heart of many diocesan priests there is an anarchic streak, and a consequent difficulty about authority. Curates live uncomfortably, sometimes, under parish priests: for them it is really durance vile. And the parish priests, when they get together, have been known to lay into the characters and behaviour of their assistants. In the vertical dimension of our common ministry there is clearly a potential for pain and unease, even if the glorious tales of the fighting 1940s and 1950s are now safely classifiable as History. No wonder, then, that our much more permanent relationship with the Bishop can also be a delicate one.

The question is, are we big enough to rise above the irritations of everyday professional life, and see the big picture? This is sketched out in *Pastores Dabo Vobis* (17):

'The ordained ministry has a radical "communitarian form", and can only be carried out as a "collective work". The Council dealt extensively with this communal aspect of the nature of priesthood, examining in succession the relationship of the priest with his own Bishop, with other priests and with the lay faithful. The ministry of priests is above all communion and a responsible and necessary co-operation with the Bishop's ministry, in concern for the universal Church and for the individual particular churches for whose service they form with the Bishop a single presbyterate.'

When Roman documents use words like 'radical' and 'necessary' they usually mean them metaphysically – 'in the very nature of things'. Priesthood not exercised in a shared way is, by definition, nonsense. With all our human limitations, of which both the Bishop and we have our share, we must resist the temptation to 'switch off' and go our own way; and if we suspect that the Bishop has mentally 'switched off' as far as we are concerned, we must exercise our genius to make sure he switches on again. Ultimately we are bound together by something bigger than temperament: our priesthood is a sharing in the priesthood and mission of the bishop (*Lumen Gentium*, 28), not a private commodity.

If a small percentage of priests in the diocese would like to prescind from the Bishop, or ostracise him, go round him, treat him like a traffic island, another small percentage would like to *be* the Bishop. So there is another question to be tackled, which is that of ambition.

A few priests will certainly think of themselves as bishop-material. They may even be told so by other people. They would be superhuman if they did not warm, at least, to the affirmation implied in this. They may imagine themselves in the seat of power, and tell themselves how much better they would handle this situation or that. How much better they would have preached that important homily. How much more sensitive they would have been in deploying their personnel. How resolute in confronting the interviewer on television. How concise and lapidary their pastoral letters would be! Bishops do not come down in a sheet from heaven, like the animals in the Acts of the Apostles. They were all ordinary priests first, and it is notorious that certain jobs (academic, curial) put you in the spotlight when the Papal Nuncio starts looking around.

1 Timothy 3:1: 'The saying is sure: whoever aspires to the office of bishop desires a noble task.' Is it wrong to be ambitious? It is certainly wrong if what you are after is simply your own vainglory. If this were your motive, and you got the job, you would (a) do it very badly, and (b) find it quite hard to get to heaven, because being a bishop would not contribute to your eternal salvation; it would distract you from it. The same arguments could be used about becoming a priest. In the old days, I mean, when adoring families and communities would

welcome you hot from your ordination ('the oils still wet on his hands') with reverence and awe, and kneel wholesale for your blessing. There was an intoxication in all that. But if what you wanted was the kudos and nothing more, you became quickly disillusioned, and you did not last the course. St Ignatius of Antioch to the Philadelphians: 'Your Bishop's office, which exists for the good of the whole community, was never obtained by his own efforts, as I know very well, nor by any other mere human agency, still less in any spirit of self-glorification.' The fact that he said this at all shows that it could have been otherwise. Even then, when being a bishop might be a short cut to a very bloody death, ambition was around.

We're talking about how the Lord runs his Church. These are not purely political decisions. The eternal salvation of souls is at stake. You don't play with that kind of stake for the sake of personal aggrandisement. You might say, 'A bishop gets a pretty frightful postbag: I wouldn't want all those complaining letters.' That's on a purely worldly level. But on a much more important level, the Bishop is responsible for the way the Gospel is preached over a wide swathe of territory, and for the provision of Mass and sacraments to tens or hundreds of thousands of people. To want to take all that on, without a very clear sign that the highest authority in the Church pressingly wished you to do so, would be presumption on a massive scale.

We must know ourselves. We spring from a society which sees it as imperative to 'get on'. Our school may have taught us that we were all destined for leadership, and that failure to achieve it would be the waste of an education. Our families may have expectations of us. Our contemporaries may all have swum effortlessly to the top, and by now be running biscuit factories and privatised railways. Our excellent degree at university may have given us cause to anticipate preferment. It is not surprising if our way of calibrating success is in terms of pips on the shoulder, purple buttons on the cassock.

Indeed, in a mild way the Church connives at this by doling out titles (canon, monsignor) to some and not to others. It makes it seem as though there were a pecking order of worth. We must know ourselves, as I say, and catch ourselves at it if we are applying the wrong criteria to the job.

In the Catholic Church, worth does not flow from rank. Nor, indeed, is it always recognised by rank. 'Remove the sandals from your feet, for the place on which you are standing is holy ground.' (Exodus 3:5.) Worth is what God recognises as worth. Worth is what produces lasting spiritual results. Worth of this kind probably belongs to the most eccentric and under-estimated priest of the diocese, who has his finger on the substance of the Catholic Faith, and succeeds in communicating it brilliantly, because, while bizarre, he is genuinely holy. In the light of eternity, only his worth will count. If you're ambitious to be like him, then that's all right.

'As in nature things move violently to their place and calmly in their place, so virtue in ambition is violent, in authority settled and calm.' Sir Francis Bacon, *Essays* – and I reckon he was right.

CHAPTER 8

The Eucharist: a journey

I was an altar-boy at the beginning of the 1950s. The '50s were construction time in Britain. There were building sites everywhere. To the north of Bedford, where I lived with my family, there was something mysterious being built called The Wind Tunnel, in which civil aircraft would be tested.

Until 1945 there had been American airmen there, and we children would cycle up through the fields to the Base and hang on the wire, until they came and tossed us packets of chewing-gum. Now, they were long gone, middle-aged executives in real estate, I suppose, in Michigan and Oregon, with England a distant memory. But we remembered them, and the nonchalant way they had put their jeeps round the corners on the country roads, and how they would joyfully buzz our houses on their way home from a successful raid.

Somewhere now, in this super-secret enclave, someone was inventing an aircraft called the Comet, of which we spoke with bated breath and great seriousness. Many of the building workers were Irish. The site, on the top of a gusty and empty hill, spawned nissen huts, mostly dormitories and canteens, and one of the canteens served on Sundays as the Catholic Chapel.

About this time, too, the Italian immigration began. We Catholics had high hopes of this. Where we lived was grimly Nonconformist, and Catholics were a tiny minority. We imagined quantities of devout and faithful families getting off the train from Rome and making straight for our churches, increasing our numbers fourfold. Perhaps the conversion of England would now start to happen in earnest? Vague memories of Luigi Gentili, Dominic Barberi, the Second Spring. We must be ready.

In fact, the families didn't arrive, but simply the menfolk. You could see them in the market on Saturdays, very short fellows with bright blue trousers and bushy moustaches. We natives were very un-European in those days. Few people went abroad for their holidays. The newcomers seemed to us like men from another planet, fascinating and yet dangerously alien. They were, to our scandal and disappointment, not addicted to Mass-going. '*Sono cattolico*,' they would say agreeably, '*ma non fanatico*'. They were engaged to work in the brickworks to the south of the town, and they too lived in camps, the ones vacated by displaced persons after the War. The bishops of Italy despatched an advance guard of clergy, to make sure that the workers were properly cared for, and our parish welcomed the first of these.

He was astonishing. I was a boy still at school, and impressionable. To begin with, this priest wasn't just a 'Father' but a 'Monsignore'. I had never met one of these. Second, his clothes were funny. He wore a strange cut of high-collared suit, or sometimes a cassock with red buttons, and he moved his hips when he walked, like a dancer, and he progressed through the workers' barracks with a sort of swagger. He talked with his hands, too, and smiled a lot, displaying all his teeth, and did a great deal of general exhorting. I went with him and watched. I had expected him to move from one man to the next and converse in a low semi-confessional voice, rather as a chaplain might in a hospital. ('Where are you from, son? Have you written to your mother? Did you make your Easter duties?') Instead he stood in the centre of each barrack and made an impassioned speech, rather like a rugby coach over the oranges at half-time, concluded with a wave of the hand which was half-salute, half-blessing, turned expertly on his heel and swirled out of the hut. A cape wrapped carelessly over the shoulders, and it would have been pure opera.

One Sunday morning, the inevitable happened. The parish priest, who was chronically short-staffed, asked the Monsignore to say Mass at the Irish construction camp, and asked me, as one of the older altar-boys, to go as his minder. A driver appeared in a muddy jeep, and hurtled us out into the countryside at reckless speed. At the point when we hit the unmade road, and he had to hang on for dear life to avoid flattening his skull on the metal roof, I thought the monsignor's smile became a little fixed. We reached the canteen, and I began to unpack the suitcase, and realised that there were no hosts.

'Altar-breads,' I said to the monsignor.

'Very good,' he said.

'There are none,' I explained.

'God bless you,' he said.

'They're not here,' I insisted, speaking slowly and moving my lips in an exaggerated way, as for a deaf person. He described an arabesque with his left hand, and beamed benignly.

'We will pray in silence,' he said, 'while you go in search of bread.'

The cook admitted to having a bicycle, so this was resurrected. As I pedalled off down the track on a ten-mile round trip, the faithful were already beginning to drift away: praying in silence was not, it seemed, their line. By the time I got back with the raw material for Mass, only a determined remnant was left.

This taught me something important, which I find still true forty-five years later. It taught me that the Eucharist has to be produced by the priest. Whatever the books say about 'presiding' – a word undreamed of in 1951 – the fact is that the priest, or someone acting for him, has to provision the Mass, has to check that the equipment is there, and that the place is ready. These days we expect this to be done by laypeople. Most of our Mass-stations are also real communities, which produce their own sacristans, and that's fine, a real advance on the days when the priest was the man to unlock the premises and set the scene.

Nine years later I was a priest, and by coincidence I was appointed to the same parish. History repeated itself. The Mass centre this time was in a village, in a British Legion hut, where I had to show up in time to let the congregation in, wipe the beer rings off the tables, open the fanlights to get rid of the smoke from the night before, and build the altar. We carried a big square altar-stone in those days, which had to go on top of the table. It was an arm-breaker of a thing, especially if you had to drag it halfway round the county on an empty stomach. My car, a 1937 Morris 12, was unreliable, and every Sunday was something of an adventure. I was distracted that Sunday. This time it was the wine that was missing from my suitcase, and this time it was too far to return to the church for supplies.

'Has anyone any wine at home?' I asked the people. There was an affronted silence.

'Perhaps,' I suggested, 'we should say the Rosary, because Mass won't be possible without any wine.' It took four mysteries to crack the man in the second row, who sullenly admitted to a bottle of Beaujolais, which he would now fetch.

Today we use Anglican churches in addition to our own, and the surroundings are aesthetic and prayerful. Often what is needed for Mass can be kept on site, and that heavy-suitcase brand of religion is rare. But wherever the celebration takes place, the priest still has to be the producer of the show, not simply the celebrant of the Mass. There is still so much to remember, even when we are on home ground, even with a well-stocked sacristy only yards away.

> Last minute names for the bidding prayers.
> A batch of tiny children to dispatch to another room at the start of Mass.
> Hymn numbers to announce.
> Readers and Eucharistic Ministers in place.
> Baskets ready for the second collection.
> Is the immobile parishioner in a wheelchair (who has communion halfway down the church) here today?

Some of this can be done by liturgy groups and sacristans.

The more the concept of 'collaborative ministry' has taken root, and ceased to be just a cliché, the better it is. It is marvellous when there is a group of layfolk in the parish who will say, in effect, 'I make myself responsible for this. Leave it to me.' This is the right way for things to be. If it is really 'my sacrifice and yours', then making the arrangements falls to all of us. But an amnesiac priest can still create havoc, rather like the conductor of an orchestra who absent-mindedly turns over two pages in the middle of a symphony. Priests are like conductors. The conductor brings in the strings and the percussion and the woodwind when they are needed, rather as we deploy catechists and servers and singers and ministers and readers. We trust that they will know their job and not need prompting. But in the last analysis, the one who presides has to make sure that the right things happen.

Well, conducting the orchestra does not make for recollection. Yes, of course, the Mass is something we celebrate with our community, and it would be absurd if we did not recognise one another's existence in the course of it: it is after all a group action, not a private luxury. There is, however, a danger that we shall become showmen, with everything done with an eye to the effect it will create. One of the sons of George III was unkindly called, by his relatives, 'Joseph Surface'. I catch myself, sometimes, being a 'Joseph Surface'. Then I remember that the Eucharist is not just a performance I put on for the people. It is supposed to enliven me, too. It is my nourishment, my inspiration and the source of my life, and I need to attend to the interior meaning of the words and actions, not just to the impression I am making. When I am talking to God, then it is God I lock on to. At that moment it is right to forget who is watching, and myself to dare to enter the Holy of Holies with all the reverence and awe I can summon. I have been most moved by those celebrations of Mass where the celebrant appeared to be lost in the truth and reality of what he was doing. Possessed by it, rather than in control of it.

I celebrate for my people, and with them. I must find a

way, however, of doing this, so that I too may be absorbed in the wonder of what is taking place. I need this as much as any parishioner. In every Mass there must be an outwardness, a real convening and animating of the assembly, but also an inwardness. It is ridiculous if the one person who can never enter into the beauty of the Mass is the priest, because his attention is dissipated and fragmented. Occasionally, in the course of my private prayer, I have an introspective moment where I ask myself, 'Just how religious am I? If it were not my professional duty to do these holy things, if it was not expected of me by hundreds of people, how much would it mean to me? Would I even go to Mass on Sundays? And is it just possible that the role has taken over from the person, so that I deliver the goods conscientiously to others, but have ceased to profit from them myself?'

We all know that sacristies before Sunday Mass can be bedlam. But it is good for me, in the sacristy or elsewhere, deliberately to create an oasis of calm and silence, and remind myself of what the Mass is.

I remember once having to preach to a group of French-speakers. I racked my rusty mental vocabulary and produced something which was halfway understandable. But afterwards a Swiss gentleman took me kindly on one side and said 'You referred to *le voyage pascal*. What a quaint expression. What did you mean?' I said that I had meant the journey Jesus made from the Last Supper, to Gethsemane, to the High Priest's house, to Pilate's palace, to Herod's palace, back to the Praetorium, down the Via Dolorosa and up the side of Calvary to his crucifixion and burial – and, of course, his resurrection. In other words, the journey from death to life.

'That's nice,' he mused, 'but unfortunately "voyage" is the term travel agents use for trips and holidays; you would hardly refer to the events of Holy Week, I think, as the Paschal Package Tour of Jesus?'

I was sorry if I had used the word for a package tour. But the underlying thought was valid. Jesus made a journey in

Holy Week, just as the Hebrews did at the Exodus. And the Mass, too, is a kind of journey. As I prepare for Mass I am conscious of the elements of death in my life. Of my own sins. Of the lamentable level of lapsation in my parish. Of the quarrels between the empire-builders in my parish. Of the difficulties experienced by my diocese. Of friends and relatives with incurable and painful illnesses. Of my own lack of ability to galvanise people into ministry of any kind, to preach convincingly, to be a Moses to this folk entrusted to me. I cannot sing. When I try, stout men turn pale. Then I realise again that the Mass is the journey from death to life, into which I can feed all these defects, personal and professional, so that every one of them is shot through with hope, and pardon. Here all the ends of my life come together: here, and only here, there is resolution, and sense is made of senseless things. The Mass turns my life from a minus into a plus. And it is a journey, not an instant transformation. I have to go through the relatively long experience of sin and weakness, bearing my own and other people's, just as Jesus was constantly on the move from the end of the Last Supper, betrayed in one place, interrogated and mocked in another, sentenced and scourged in a third. It was a long, dark night and day of suffering and humiliation. All this, with his death on the cross, was the stuff which the resurrection would redeem.

When I am at Mass, I live this passage from death to life, and contribute my own sixpennyworth of bewilderment and suffering, hand it in, so to speak, that he may transform it. I must never allow my interaction with the people in church, however liturgically right and proper, to take this away from me.

What is true of the Mass is true of the Blessed Sacrament in an empty church. Here is the Lord who will take me on the journey from death to life. He says, 'I am the way.' He is the way to the Father: that's the journey I have to make, home to the Father. The Father is the source of sense. He is truth, and reality. He is the is-ness of things. He is the opposite of fantasy and delusion. He is substance and fact, my fortress, my rock where I can take refuge, my shield, my mighty help, my stronghold. My journey from death to life is a rescue from the Big Lie, which says that it all depends on me.

The Eucharist has been an abiding presence in my life, from those very utilitarian Masses in grubby bars and cafés in the Home Counties, to house-Masses in South American shanties, to tiny tabernacles I have seen in the Sahara, to the Pope's Mass in Wembley Stadium in the paralysing heat, when we priests concelebrated with pieces of newspaper on our heads to stop us getting sunstroke. The Lord has always been there like the core in my cable, saying, 'Join me on my journey.' By the Eucharist he puts the frame round my picture and defines it. My life is not just a chaotic jumble of happiness and sadness, arbitrarily mixed, and to be arbitrarily terminated at some time in the future, devoid of sense or meaning, somebody's capricious joke. It is the journey of a disciple who is following his Master home.

CHAPTER 9

Belonging

The First Communion group in our parish did its first 'module' recently. They were invited to reflect, these seven- and eight-year-olds, on their experience of *belonging*. You can see the thinking behind this. The Eucharist is to be for them in years to come not only a means of personal union with Jesus, but also the bond which draws them in charity to their fellow-Christians. We were teaching them, in an infantile way, that 'The Eucharist makes the Church'. They were taking on board what *Lumen Gentium* says: 'Strengthened by the body of Christ in the eucharistic communion, they manifest in a concrete way that unity of the People of God which this holy sacrament aptly signifies and admirably realises.' (LG, 11.) They were learning the two senses of 'communion'. We receive the Body of Christ in order to become the Body of Christ.

This is all very well, until you begin to think of their impoverished experience of 'belonging'. We presume, in our catechetical books, that there's a family out there: a providing father, a loving and nurturing mother, a clutch of brothers and sisters. But a frightening number of these children with only one parent live in a tiny flat. All traditional notions of 'extended family' are quite simply out of sight. Aunts, uncles, cousins are nowhere on the scene: a granny, perhaps, but that's the sum total. Modern families are brittle, fragile, and extremely nuclear. There seems to be a centrifugal force which tears them apart, and makes blood-relations strangers to one another. If we are saying to these children, 'Holy Communion will make you more deeply God's family, grouped around his table, just like your family at home', we may be talking about old-fashioned Sunday lunch to someone who has only eaten baked beans off a tray in front of the TV. It's like talking of the fatherhood of God to a child who has never had a father, who has a drunk and abusive father, or who has had a succession of fathers.

So analogies, like family and fatherhood, have a limited shelf-life, and must be used with due caution. As for the children, so for us. Being a diocesan priest means you belong, concretely, to a territory and a group of people. All the people of the diocese, in fact, have a claim upon us, but we belong in a particular way to the bishop and the other priests with whom we serve, and they belong to us. Inevitably, we use the examples of 'family' or 'fraternity' to express the ideal. But our skill in creating a warm, welcoming, fraternal presbyterate in our diocese will depend to a large extent on our other experiences of belonging and of brotherhood: on the quality of our family life before we ever thought of priesthood; on the quality of our relationships at school, at university, in our first workplace. Do we actually know what 'belonging' should feel like? What sacrifices should I be prepared to make for the general happiness and well-being of the presbyterate of my diocese? What sacrifices should the others make in order that I may be happy? What is the right proportion of give-and-take? If we have no previous personal history of harmonious, unselfconscious, fruitful belonging, it will be hard to know. There will be much to learn. We may have to experiment, and we shall make mistakes.

A university professor said to me recently, about his students – to whom he was very attached – 'They are all Thatcher's children.' He meant by this that they were competitive, perfectionist, extremely hardworking, acquisitive, very much aware of their entitlements, and to a large extent loners. He was not criticising them or blaming them. He was simply reflecting on the shift in culture which had taken place in his own lifetime. Well, we are all children of our culture. If we belong to different generations, that may mean different cultures, different fundamental assumptions about the sheer business of living, and living among others. I am labouring this point because unless we understand it, and have insight into it, and are therefore merciful and patient, we will never be gentle with ourselves, and we will judge others harshly. 'Belonging' as a diocesan quality will always need working at, and there will be accidents and setbacks along the way, because in trying to bring it about we are acting in a way which is, now, profoundly counter-cultural.

Pastores Dabo Vobis quotes the decree *Presbyterorum Ordinis* of Vatican II, and says: 'The Presbyterate, in the fullness of its truth, is a *mysterium*. It is in fact a supernatural reality *because it is rooted in the sacrament of Holy Orders*. The Sacrament of Holy Orders is conferred upon each of (us) as individuals, but (we) are inserted into the communion of the Presbyterate.' And later in the same paragraph, 'Presbyterate thus appears as a true family, as a fraternity whose ties do not arise from flesh and blood but *from the grace of Holy Orders*.' So the sum total of the priests of my diocese adds up to an entity in its own right, a new thing, something more than the sum of its parts, something sacramental. This is all very well, as a theological statement. But Holy Orders will not create fraternity, as if by magic. We've got to work at it, and be forgiving, both with ourselves and with one another. Ordination is not so much a magic cement, as a motivation for this constant and faithful effort. If we are the kind of people who take offence at the words and deeds of others, and freeze them off for all eternity, our presbyterate does not stand a chance. It is unavoidable, isn't it, if we share houses, and parishes, and chaplaincies, and work together in deaneries and working parties and commissions, that from time to time we shall annoy and disappoint one another. I think it is vital that we decide in advance that no wound shall be regarded as mortal, because in fact we are all mortals, and fallible, and we all need second chances.

Lumen Gentium (para 26) has a fascinating reflection on the identity and nature of the Diocese. It's talking about the 'local Church' and it says: 'This Church of Christ is really present in all legitimately organised local groups of the faithful, which, in so far as they are united to their pastors, are also quite appropriately called Churches in the New Testament.' In other words, just as a scientist can take a piece of DNA and predicate, from the tiny cell he has, the qualities of the whole organism, so the whole supernatural *mysterium* of the Church is present in all the dioceses, one by one (and to quote *LG* again) 'though they may be often small and poor, or existing in the diaspora'. So this is true of East Anglia, and Menevia, and Aberdeen, and Plymouth, and all the rest of them: the whole *mysterium* of Christ pitching his tent among men, moving among them as the Good Shepherd, being the true vine, constructing his Temple out of living stones – all of this, not just part of it, comes true in each of these concrete communities. You and I, being priests, are part of this *mysterium*. The theology of the Church is verified in us, because we belong to this particular presbyterate.

So let's think of the concrete reality of our own diocese, whichever it may be. Our belonging began, formally and canonically, when we were incardinated. For those from traditions other than the Catholic one, like our newly arrived ex-Anglican brethren, this will be a novel concept, the idea that a priest signs articles, so to speak, with a particular bishop, and all things being equal remains in the presbyterate of that bishop (or his successor) for the rest of his life. Just as a monk, once professed in an abbey, can identify with some certainty the place of his eventual grave, so I, at the recent ordination of my new bishop, looked at him and thought to myself, 'In all probability, that is the man who will bury me.' That's what incardination means.

In our sourer moments we may think that incardination is nothing more than a canonical device for pinning us down. Well, it's up to us: if we withhold our heart, so to speak, and keep our brother priests at arm's length, reducing them to professional colleagues, then incardination remains a legal concept and nothing more.

It takes place these days at ordination to the diaconate. Years ago, if I remember correctly, it was a separate little ceremony which happened just before the conferring of the tonsure (of which today's equivalent is 'candidacy'). I recall my own with some difficulty. It was in the Presbytery at Thetford in 1955, and I had to kneel down by Bishop Parker's armchair and swear something or other which escapes me now. All I can remember is the pattern on the carpet. At the time I had no notion of the importance of what I was doing. I was, in effect, acquiring a family. Whether the old Bishop saw it like this, I'm not so sure. I suspect he was more concerned with laying claim to his chickens and fencing them in securely so that no one – neither another bishop nor Her Majesty's Armed Forces – could steal them from him. The accent in those days was very one-sided, emphasising obedience on the part of the subject without any corresponding duty being incurred by the superior. In fact, this was one of the most significant acts of my life.

So it's throwing in your lot, for better or worse, with a partic-ular bishop, and with a particular bunch of men. They may not be the men you would have chosen as companions for yourself. But in concrete fact, these are the men God has given you to love. These are the men to whom, under God, you owe your loyalty. Even if you are seconded to other work on the other side of the world, as a missionary in the Andes, for instance, or as a military chaplain in Bosnia, or a *minutante* in the Vatican, you remain part of their family, and they part of yours.

Diocesan priests do not have a vocation to live in community. If we had, we should have become religious. For the religious, the act of belonging to a community is a spiritual factor of great importance. Even if a religious works in a parish, his centre of gravity is in his community. The duty of charity to the brothers with whom he lives is a prime element in his vocation; just as important, if not more so, than the diligence with which he cares for his parishioners.

Well, we diocesan priests are not called to community. But

we *are* called to fraternity. This means that God expects us to treat each other not sentimentally – God save us from that – but still supportively and patiently, with generosity, with humour, and with great and warm charity. The instinct which impels us to do this is not very different from that which made Italian, Irish and Polish families, disembarking in New York at the turn of the century, and living in the most cramped conditions, move over and make room for their brothers and cousins who arrived on the boat the following year. Blood is thicker than water, they would have said. Well, belonging to a diocese has something of the same quality. The priests of my diocese (or yours) might be eccentric, cantankerous, crotchety, mercurial, open to criticism from so many points of view. This is the enduring miracle of the Incarnation, that Jesus Christ, having lived thirty-three years among people just like this, continues to do so now, in the Church which is his Body.

The presbyterate of each diocese has its own character, and its own characters. It has its own jokes. It has its own collective memories. Doing retreats up and down the country has taught me how different dioceses can be, as different as Balkan republics. My own diocese is a new one, and its presbyterate is thus recently formed, and the founder members of it have had a share in shaping it, deciding what it will be like, what its overall tone will be, what kind of atmosphere will prevail in it. One day all of us, from old dioceses or new, will find our way into the back of our diocesan yearbooks where the names of the dead appear in italics. There are legends there – in mine, names like 'William Wareing' who was transmuted from a Vicar Apostolic into a real bishop, in 1850, and had an area about the size of Belgium to care for with just a handful of priests; 'Provost Husenbeth' and 'Canon Seth Eccles'. One day I shall be one with Canon Seth Eccles, and William Wareing, and the redoubtable Provost, and then the living members of the diocesan priesthood will pray for us, and remember us at Mass, as we remember before God the members of our own families. In the Catholic Church, belonging to a diocese is serious stuff.

CHAPTER 10

Centre of gravity

In the medieval folklore of the Church, comparisons are often made between the worldly secular clergy, with their eye to the main chance, and the unworldly friars, with their purified and unselfish apostolate.

Well, we *are* worldly. This doesn't mean we are intent, most of us, on feathering our own nests. Diocesan priesthood offers few opportunities of that. But it does mean that our concerns are with the world, with the *saeculum*, and that if we become holy we do so precisely by our involvement in it.

Clearly, the world is a dangerous place. You need only read St John's letters, or watch the TV news, to realise that. So much of the piety we have been taught has said to us, 'As far as possible, flee the world. Create your own basis of holiness as a man apart. This will insulate you against the temptations the world will offer.' This is because we have borrowed our spirituality from traditions based on religious life. And the religious has his centre of gravity in his community, in his Rule, in the Constitutions of his Order. He may be asked to work in a parish setting, and he may do it superbly well. England is particularly rich in religious who are splendid parish priests. But against the background of the original charism of his community, such work is probably exceptional, and it may set up tensions for the individual.

For me as a diocesan priest, the world outside the presbytery and the church is my natural habitat. I walk it with confidence. I am at home in it. My centre of gravity is there, in the streets and the houses. If the world is a moral and social jungle, then I am like a seasoned hunter who handles it with a sure touch. I do not share its values. But I talk and understand its language.

My spiritual growth stems, at least in part, from this. I am like a car battery which charges itself up when the car is running. There is a creative friction between myself and the people of my parish which energises me. I learn from them. I watch how they handle poverty, bereavement, suffering, and I admire them. When they come to confession, I appreciate the depth of their difficulties, and their courage in confronting them. Far from being Mr Stainless-Steel, watching the great unwashed from a distance and patronising them, I feel for them and with them. With them I sometimes feel that the world of moral theology manuals is very far away. It isn't that I want to argue, or quarrel with the principles they spell out. It's simply that I wish the professors would acknowledge the problems under which ordinary people labour. Sometimes the experts remind you of Miss Pole in Mrs Gaskell's *Cranford*, who delivers herself, at a tea party, of some sweeping statements about Men, and concludes, 'My father was a man, and I know the sex pretty well.' Do the boffins know my people pretty well? Some of them do, because they too have done time 'on the beat'. But some of them don't.

What spirituality is best adapted to this chaotic lifestyle? Is spirituality the same as prayer? There will be days when I don't pray formally. I will have been woken by the phone. There will have been a small pile of bills to pay and letters to answer. There will have been a Mass in the church and then a school Mass, with a teacher wanting a quiet conversation afterwards about a family problem. There will have been an urgent hospital visit. There will have been a funeral, maybe at a distance, with relatives to talk to. There will have been a quick raid on Sainsbury's to stock up the freezer (who has housekeepers these days?), and, of course, more parishioners leaping out from behind the dog-food and wanting a quick word. There will have been a couple of plausible tramps at the door, and a clutch of messages and exasperated sighs on the answerphone. And finally to crown the day, there will have been an interminable school governors' meeting ('to squeeze the budget, Father'). I get home at ten or half-past and realise that I have said no Office, and that there has been no quiet reflective prayer in my day. I have the impression that I woke up running, and have not stopped running since.

On the surface, a defective day. I should have planned it better. I should have ring-fenced time for prayer. Perhaps, if I had had my wits about me, I could have done so. My weakness is that I don't plan enough; I simply respond as generously as I can to stimuli. I am like a juggler throwing batons in the air and catching them again. If I can get to the end of the day without dropping one (breaking an appointment, forgetting an interview, losing my temper) I think, 'I've done pretty well.' And then I remember, with a guilty start, 'But I didn't pray.' So I say to myself, 'Tomorrow I will pray.'

And, usually, I do. The contours of the next day are different. I find the energy to get up early. Or there is a fallow period which I can use. Maybe I have to say to the Lord, ruefully, 'Sero, sero te amavi . . . Late have I loved thee', but I do it with the clear certainty that he understands. It seems to me that I must make sure – honestly sure – not that I have an infallible routine, but that there is sufficient prayer in my life. He has put me here to care for people, and people are not neat and tidy in their needs and demands. And when finally I am alone before the Lord, I cannot shut out all that human experience. If the stories I've heard, the intuitions I have about people, are strong and insistent, then probably the best thing I can do is make them part of my prayer rather than let them become wasp-like distractions.

That preceding day, the over-full one, was not a spiritual waste. I met – including the phone and the post, the school and the funeral, several hundred people. I brought to them the love that is in me, and my own idiosyncratic witness to the goodness and pardon of God. With varying success, I listened attentively to them, tried to enter into their way of thinking and assessing situations, trying to bring the Gospel to bear, rather than lecturing severely and from a height. I was enriched by those people. Although I was dog-tired at the end of the day, my battery was charged. With luck, the day when I do manage to pray will be a Thursday, and I shall be able to say, with conviction, at Compline, 'The lot marked out for me is my delight: welcome indeed the heritage that falls to me.'

That mutual enrichment is imperceptible. I only appreciate the depth of it when it is time to move on to a new appointment, and I realise how painful it is to say 'goodbye' to so many folk. It is a real goodbye, because when it comes to staying in touch with hundreds of friends, by phone or by post, the flesh is weak, and I know that a Christmas card is as much as I shall manage. Painful for them, but for me too. We have grown together, in spite of hiccups and criticisms. We have got to know one another's ways, strengths and blind spots, and have learned to make allowances. In the early days of computer games there was a creature called, I think, the Pacman. He was really an animated mouth. He worked his way across the screen biting lumps out of whatever he met, giving it a new shape. In the nicest way, we all give one another a new shape, we form one another, I hope not by biting, but by knocking the corners off, teaching, moulding.

So the version of me which presents himself for judgement when my life ends will be a version with other people's fingerprints all over it: the people's fingerprints, parishioners' fingerprints. They will all have had a share in producing the final article. In this way I shall bring them all with me, and God will judge me in the context of them, because, Lord, I shall want to say, this is where my centre of gravity was, this is where you put it, when you called me to be a diocesan priest.

CHAPTER 11

Between a rock and a hard place

When I was working in Cambridge, Cardinal Ratzinger came to town.

Cardinal Ratzinger was the Church's doctrinal expert. He was in charge of that department in the Vatican which ensures that the Catholic Faith is taught correctly. This made him, in a way, the Church's watchdog, since he was protecting its inheritance, its 'deposit of faith'. He had come, by invitation, to give a lecture in the University.

I had been a student in Rome, many years before. My memories of the Cardinals then, who performed great ceremonies on feastdays, were of old men, remote as porcelain statues, who were escorted everywhere by soldiers resembling Napoleon's Imperial Guard, and almost lifted up and down the steps. But this was another brand of Cardinal. He was alert, intelligent, well turned-out, spick and span, a bandbox Cardinal with all his wits about him, who walked tall and conducted himself with dignity, who could cope in several languages and tangle with the toughest theologians Cambridge could deploy.

The lecture hall was packed. Ratzinger was renowned as a great disciplinarian: books censured and censored, theologians warned off, negative verdicts passed on emotive issues like the spread of liberation theology and the Anglican-RC unity talks. In the liberal atmosphere of an English university, a visit from such an unreconstructed and notorious conservative was a considerable draw.

He spoke about a concept which for most of those present was double-Dutch: the existence of a natural moral law. He took as his starting-point the spread of the drug culture, and the burgeoning of terrorism throughout the world. Analysing them he pointed out that, however distortedly, even these expressed the strivings of the human spirit, yearnings of the soul for a short-cut paradise, a religious enthusiasm perverted to earthly concerns. Beneath them, he said, we can detect a new longing for what is absolute, and total: even, on their own terms, 'moral'.

I won't go into the detail of the talk. It was very learned, and closely reasoned. It was also, in an intellectual way, quite confrontational. As they used to say outside the pubs on beery evenings, it was 'fighting talk', even if monotonously read. The Cardinal gave no quarter to the positivists. It was a cerebral punch-up, in which he was very much at home. He didn't need protecting. He relished the argumentative atmosphere of the University. He didn't shelter behind rank, or uniform, or title. He welcomed spontaneous questions.

It wasn't pure abstraction. He did talk about drugs and terrorism. But his main drift was his certainty that there is an objective natural moral law, making demands on all of us. When all was said and done he was doing his job, which was to patrol the uplands of ethics and morality, and make valid comments about what underlay moral attitudes in the modern world. Given those parameters, he seemed to me to be doing a good job. It made sense to me. I couldn't fault what he said. Others, more erudite, might.

But while he was doing his job, I, as a diocesan priest, had to do mine. I was painfully aware that two or three miles from where the lecture took place, there were housing estates where the City sent their problem families. Square miles of peeling flats and semi-detached houses where life was based on different premises. There were alcoholics, and addicts, and people with records for GBH, and folk who simply couldn't pay the rent. There were people in promiscuous, shifting relationships. The burglary rate was high. Many of these folk had huge gas-guzzling bangers churning the grass verge outside their homes; some of them had Alsatians and Rottweilers. They spent more on dog-food and petrol than they would on a brace of kids. There were eccentric old widows and widowers there who had barricaded themselves into squalid apartments and fetid kitchens and never opened the door. Their only company was the TV and perhaps a mangy cat. They had retired from the human race, having found it wanting.

For many of these, life was just a series of staccato incidents, a mixture of good luck and bad luck; not much cause and effect. Their approach to life was existential, and they dealt with each new set of circumstances as it arose. Immutable principles and inviolable laws didn't figure in their reckoning. Indeed, the idea of anything being immutable or inviolable was a laugh. Every standard had to bend under the weight of immediate need, just as every public official or policeman probably had his price if you could pitch your bribe correctly. Rules could be bent; that was what they were there for.

I was the only person at the lecture who belonged to both worlds. My formation was the same as the Cardinal's. Like him, I had been trained to deal in essences and natures, in the infinite and the eternal. Words like 'intrinsic' came trippingly off my lips. Scholastic philosophy had left an indelible mark on me, as had the theology of the time before Vatican II. I believed in an objective pattern of doctrine and morality and a Church with the right to teach them. Otherwise I could not have gone on being a priest. If I had had to concoct my own Creed from my own reading of Scripture and the leadings of my heart, I should have left. So I wasn't quarrelling with the Cardinal. I was simply wondering, 'How relevant is all this to the people on the estate?' Now some people would say that if we had harder-working and more prayerful priests, whole areas of cities like the one I describe could be converted to correct Catholicism. I don't believe this. I think it is the lot of the Church to be a little flock. While preaching what we believe, we have at the same time to accept that most of the world is never going to accept what we say. A bit more zeal on my part would not topple these folk over into reimbursing those from whom they had stolen their cars, submitting their serial marriages to annulment tribunals, throwing away their condoms, refraining from making false claims on the Social Security, giving up lager, lining up outside the local church for Sunday Mass, taking on board the Church's social teaching, joining CAFOD projects and teaching their children to say the Angelus. These families and individuals are who they are, and are as they are, and they are mostly not going to change very much, and there are thousands and thousands of them, and they are lovable, and they are real. And I, as a diocesan priest, belong to them, and to a large extent understand them. I belong to their world as well as to the Ratzinger world.

Where I am is best described as the place between the general and the particular. It is an uncomfortable place to be. It is the vocation of the diocesan priest to occupy that space, without trying to escape from it. He could escape into the particular – he could identify himself so much with cause of the people on the estate that he develops a great contempt for Church attitudes and principles. He could escape into the general, and stay at home reading theological works because involvement with the unchurched masses is too upsetting. To remain in the middle, and to be loyal to both ends of the spectrum, is what we are called to do – and often it hurts, and is painful.

One of my favourite meditation passages is the one in John 10 where Jesus says, 'I am the gate.' I have often put this saying together with others from the same Gospel – 'I am the way, the truth and the life; no one can come to the Father except through me.' (John 14:6.) 'No one has ever seen God; it is the only Son, who is nearest to the Father's heart, who has made him known.'(John 1:18.) Jesus is the gateway to the Father.

By himself the Father is inscrutable, unknowable; St John of the Cross is adamant about this. Only by faith can he be known, by the dark and helpless faith which turns its back on all conventional ways of knowing people. Our faith is focused entirely on the Son of Man, who is God's self-expression, his only clue, held out to us. It is as though he were saying, 'If you want to know what I'm like, then look at this man. In his human way of being – if you have the faith to grasp it correctly – you will have a hint of me, the ground of your being, the founder of everything that makes sense, the fount of true meaning.' If God the Father contains within himself every-thing that is true, and real, and durable, then I want to feast my mind and my heart upon him. And he says to me, 'If you want to do that, then use the gate. My Son is the gateway to me. Absorb his Gospel and make it your own, and you will have found me.'

There have been days when I have even looked at the doors of the tabernacle and seen them as the gate. It is somehow through this mystery, the mystery of the Eucharist, that I have access to the Truth which underlies all appearances. It is a Truth in front of which I can only sit with my mouth open, catching fugitive glimpses of something totally beyond me. (It is significant that the doors of the tabernacle are closed.) If I begin my day by immersing myself in this reality, I can manage all the semi-realities and pretences which will cross my path in the course of it. 'Da robur, fer auxilium.' Stiffen me, Lord, with what is genuine and indestructibly solid, sound and right, before I address the world of shadows and deceits (including my own).

'I am the gate; anyone who enters through me will be safe.' Does it seem that Our Lord is the way through into an enclosed space, where things are all right? No wolves inside these fortifications? Is it like a vootrekkers' laager, at the heart of which God dwells? If so, there is a whole civilisation of love inside this sheepfold, and how right I am to queue up at the gate of it, waiting my turn, asking Christ to lead me through. And I am right, too, to recognise so many friends in the gateway with me, both living and dead, so that my prayer is not just a private thing, but embraces my parish and my family and hundreds of other people too. Be the gate, Lord, for all of us. Lead us to the Father. John 14:8: Philip said,

'Lord, let us see the Father and then we shall be satisfied.' 'Have I been with you all this time,' said Jesus to him, 'and still you do not know me?' My prayer is a yearning to know, not just on my own behalf, but bringing with me the unconscious prayers of many.

John 17:3: And eternal life is this: to know you, the only true God, and Jesus Christ whom you have sent.

I believe this is correct imagery, but only as far as it goes. It goes wrong when you confuse it with the traditional models of the Church which say that she is the One Ark of Salvation for All, the Fortress, the Perfect Society, inside whose walls you will be safe; outside is the howling wilderness, where you will emphatically not be safe. I can too easily elide the Sheepfold of St John with the Church's juridical picture of herself, and say that only in the bosom of Holy Mother Church will I find the Father.

If I do this, what am I saying about the men and women on the estate? That they have no access to the Father? Or even more sinisterly, that the Father has no access to them? That because they do not believe in a natural moral law, and do not live by the filigree of rules and truths which govern life inside the Church, they are cut off from the source of meaning, and truth, and reality? That I can't believe. It would remind me too much of the Jansenist crucifix where Our Lord's arms are only half-outstretched, because in effect he did not die for all. No, this is the Lord who had compassion on the multitude. He didn't wait for them to show signs of conformity before having compassion. If he only died for the ones who live by the rules, then the Redemption was singularly ineffective, and highly elitist.

The gate in the wall of the sheepfold is not just the way in. It is also the way out. He says it, doesn't he? 'Anyone who enters through me will be safe: he will go safely in and out, and be sure of finding pasture.' Maybe it is God's will that today I should discover him *outside* the sheepfold, dwelling peaceably among his bizarre and eccentric people, pasturing them in his own way. The single mothers working 'on the black', the illegal immigrants, the characters on the bench by the station with cans of Special Brew, the bored graffiti-boys, the council house tenants with secret lodgers, the agnostic comprehensive teacher struggling resentfully with a school assembly, the earnest Jehovah's witness with pebble-glasses and buck teeth, the joyriders in the souped-up Escort. All miles away from the Church. But to them I am sent, because I am a diocesan priest. I am sent through the gate, who is Christ. I am sent from the inside out, not from the outside in, and he introduces me to the Father in the most unlikely places.

It is still uncomfortable, occupying the space between the general and the particular, between the rock and the hard place. It is uncomfortable to belong to a world of orthodoxy, and yet spend so much of my time and energy with the unorthodox, and indeed to belong to their world too. I would want to say to men preparing for diocesan priesthood that this divided heart is the characteristic pain of their vocation, and if they experience the pain, it is a sign that they will be good priests. We are pinned with the Lord to the Cross, who 'has made the two into one, and broken down the barrier which used to keep them apart, actually destroying in his own person the hostility caused by the rules and decrees of the Law.' (Ephesians 2:14.)

CHAPTER 12

Never quite

During almost forty years of priesthood, I have as often as not replaced men of unusual ability or had such men as colleagues. This is at the same time a privilege and a disaster.

The hardest act to follow is that of the pastoral visitor. My uncle, a priest for forty-two years, was like this. He was the priest who knew his district, knew his parish, like the back of his hand, who visited every household at least twice a year, and was in fact everyone's favourite uncle. With economy of movement and time, he spent parts of evenings in hundreds of houses, without anyone feeling short-changed or hard done by. He did this with such ease that it was disguised as leisure. I know that in describing this I might seem to be writing ironically, sarcastically, but indeed I am not. I admire it from afar, genuinely and sincerely, but also with a kind of helplessness. When I try to do it, I get caught up by the first or second family I meet, and spend so much time with them that there is none left for anyone else. Or I walk in halfway through *Coronation Street* and realise how unwelcome I am. Or remember, with cold panic, an appointment back at the presbytery. Or just, to be honest, lose heart.

So I spend my life comparing myself, to my disadvantage, with various priests. Others also are comparing. 'Father X,' said an old Polish lady reproachfully, 'is every week coming in mine house, and is eating with me one egg.' In the matter of ovular ingestion I run a poor second, and will always be a disappointment to the punters. 'Do you know all the scores from the Test Matches for the last five years?' says the boy. 'No one could,' I answer loftily, 'It's impossible.' 'Father X did,' he says, wistfully.

Father X, while spending 120 hours a week in people's houses, managed also to be chaplain to his local school, with frequent visits to one or two non-Catholic ones thrown in. He was elegantly present in the playground and genuinely befriended hundreds of children, whose names he never forgot (and whom he had met at home, anyway, the night before), but also taught the odd class, with real panache, so that they clamoured for him to come back. When I go to school I end up standing on one leg on windy, rainswept open spaces, acutely self-conscious, while the youngsters live their life round me as if I were an inconvenient tree left behind by the planners. I forget children's names and have to ask, with assumed brazenness, 'Remind me who you are,' and can read the disappointment in their faces.

Father Y had a way with tramps which put me to shame. I would feel threatened by them, and completely at a loss whether to believe their stories or not. In the end I would either take a stand and say, 'I'm sorry, I can't help you,' and blench under the inevitable torrent of abuse ('Call yerself a Christian?'); or give them a couple of quid to go away; or (occasionally) be taken for a monumental ride, and pay someone's fare to Aberdeen or Jersey or Lisnaskea where his only brother was dying of AIDS compounded by starvation, bilharzia and ptomaine poisoning; with a bit thrown in for a meal on the way. Father Y, on the other hand, had an instinctive hunch about the right thing to do. He would know the tramp's name, and remember it. He never lost his temper. He would know whom to ring in Aberdeen or Jersey or Lisnaskea, to verify the story. Homeless men he would bundle into his baby Fiat and whisk away into the town, where an adoring landlady would accommodate them in her B and B. He had a sort of affinity with tramps. The chancers and the con-men he would laugh, not at, but with. The genuine cases of distress he would help in a practical way, and they never forgot him. I probably gave away more money than he did, but with a bad grace: by comparison I came across as severe, standoffish, on a short fuse, and (if truth be told) very insecure.

Father Z was musical. 'Oh what a delight,' carolled the parishioners at the end of Mass, 'to hear such a lovely voice. And hasn't he trained the choir well? And the orchestra! All those youngsters with their instruments! Wasn't the saxophone divine? A real pleasure, now, coming to Mass.' Having sown demon seeds of jealousy in my ignoble breast, they drove home for Sunday lunch. They may, or may not, know that the first time I sang Mass, the sanctuary lamp broke – it splintered spontaneously and poured oil all over the Canon's carpet. When, in default of a deacon last Easter, I volunteered to sing the Exsultet (and practised for weeks) someone walked out during the Vigil. When I attempted to practise a new piece of music with a congregation, I was taken aside very kindly by a retired major-general, who said, 'Father, we love and respect you very much, but my personal advice is to give it a rest, what?'

At the end of a day, however, no diocesan priest, even Fathers X or Y, let alone Z, can say, 'I have done it all, the job is finished, there is nothing left over.' There will always be something left over, as long as there are families in the parish who have lost their faith, or don't practise it any more; so long as there are folk in need of the Gospel and not finding it. So all of us will go to bed with a sense of unfinished business. If my job is not in a parish, but on a marriage tribunal, there are always cases pending, there is work on the spike awaiting attention. If I work in education there are always more imaginative ways to devise of teaching children or training catechists. If I work in a seminary there is always something else I should read, some article or some book recently published, so that the courses I give will be more complete and up-to-date. In other words, however talented you may be, if you are a perfectionist who needs to round things off and draw a line which means 'dealt with', you had better not be a diocesan priest.

Now at its worst, this awareness can produce a sense of weariness and failure. Even if I am phenomenally gifted, I never quite measure up to my own expectations. It is as though some degree of failure were built into the fabric of my job; failure, my own and other people's, is my stock-in-trade. This feeling of failure needs bringing out into the open, it needs addressing.

It must be said. There is a shadow-side which is part of the texture of priesthood. Right at the heart of the most sacred thing we do is a reference to failure. 'This is the cup of my blood, the blood of the new and everlasting covenant, which will be shed for you and for all, so that sins may be forgiven.' Sins. My job is about sins. My principal task in the course of the day is to bring the healing power of Christ's Passion to bear on human failure. If there were no human failure, would I be out of a job? The Sacrament of Reconciliation is tucked quite unselfconsciously into the Church's repertoire of treasures. It is as though the Church were taking for granted our periodic, cyclic failure. Cheerfully she sets about dealing with it. It is moving to see how sometimes a recent convert to the Catholic Church will arrange to come to confession almost with shame and apology, as if appalled by the fact that it's necessary. The born Catholic is more nonchalant about sin. From the earliest days in our Catholic primary school, sin has been a familiar concept; human failure is part of the furniture of our spiritual lives.

We are very hard-headed when it comes to money, and buildings. We build a new church for the number of people we anticipate will use it. We don't build for the total number of baptised Catholics in the district, expecting that one day they will wake up to their obligations, and present themselves for Sunday Mass. If, one Sunday, they did, we should be floored, for we could not accommodate them. In the same way we arrange our Mass times with an eye to reality. We do not advertise as many Masses for a Holiday of Obligation as we do for a Sunday, because we know the people will not be there. In so far as Mass-going can be said to mean success (an impossibly limited concept, of course), we actually build and plan for failure.

The other day a mother met me about her daughter's confirmation. Or, rather, about her non-confirmation. 'She won't think of it, Father,' she said, 'If she gets confirmed, the other girls in the class won't give her a moment's peace, she'll be finished.' She described how mortified the lass had been when some of her mates spotted her going to Mass one Saturday night. She had experienced real shame, as though she had been photographed in a red-light district. If I look down my church on a Sunday and see many blue-rinses and bald heads, but hardly any adolescents, I now know why. Catholic youngsters have created a culture in which you keep church-going under your hat, like a guilty secret. They actively prevent one another from practising their faith. Heaven knows what they think and feel when I appear in their school corridors between lessons, or in the kitchen when they get home for tea. All this can make me feel very responsible, and very futile. My generation of clergy is the first one to fail so signally to attract or inspire young people. It's failure on a massive scale.

I list these examples, but not because I really believe that they indicate personal failure. My hard head tells me that there are so many historical and sociological factors at play, not only in my parish, but all over Britain, and Western Europe, and North America. I cannot take all this on my own shoulders, all this shift and change, as though I were personally to blame. It would be quite absurd for me to do so. And, as the parishioners point out very charitably, we can't all be Pavarotti. If I'm not a raging extrovert, that's all right. There are compensations! I am not accountable for the media, or for changes in educational method, or in the social mores which take it for granted that everyone will be sexually active at sixteen. I just happen to have been ordained at this time, and to be this sort of person.

However, in parallel to this emphatic, sensible, accurate, reasonable self, there exists another one, the one who wakes up at two in the morning and to whom the whole scene is immediately and appallingly present, at its bleakest. There is a pitiless and unreasonable piece of me which says, 'You should be doing something about all this, and you aren't, either because you are too lazy, or too stupid.'

I suspect that I have echoed fairly accurately what some priests, at least, feel, even if they never give voice to their feelings. We have, so many of us, bought the package of excellence, achievement and efficiency. Well, as I said, I do not believe that all this indicates personal failure. I'm echoing it here in order to refute it. I believe that priesthood is so sublime and splendid a thing that it has little or nothing to do with personal performance or effectiveness. Yes, of course we do our best to care for the flock entrusted to us and, yes, we do our utmost to work collaboratively with the People of God as it lives out its baptismal priesthood, if that doesn't sound too politically correct. But the bit of input we manage, whether we are incredibly gifted or frankly mediocre, counts for very little beside the theological and spiritual reality of what we are, who we are privileged to be.

I was thinking the other day about that passage at the beginning of Mark, where Jesus gets up very early in the morning and leaves the house, and goes up the mountain to a deserted place where he can pray. I tried to imagine what the prayer of Christ was like, and compare it with my own. He was Father-centred in a way that I can never be. His whole humanity was lived in reference to the Father. He must have fallen into prayer with a sense of colossal relief. Communing with the Father was so real and so natural for him. Christ prayed out of a humanity which was straight, unsullied, uncorrupted, uninhibited, unhampered. As man, he could wordlessly profess his utter dependence on the Father, his love of him, his need of him, with an intensity which I can only imagine.

When I pray, on the other hand, I pray out of a humanity which has been warped by sin and diffidence and laziness. If there were prayer-stakes, and this were a competitive matter, I would need a very large handicap. When I pray, I have huge distractions. Could I use this idea in a sermon, or an article? Why didn't I find the words to wither the person who snubbed me on Thursday? I can find them now. Can anyone see me praying? What do they think? What's the time, and have I completed the period of prayer I set myself in order to feel virtuous? Between the distractions there will be good patches, when I focus on the Lord with sincerity, but not many. Mind, it isn't a lost cause. My prayer does improve, with the months and the years. And none of it is wasted, I know, not even the distractions, because I pray with honesty and faith. But I'm a poor hand at it, and that's the truth.

Then I think of God the Father, not in the least meaning to be irreverent, as if he were a short-wave radio enthusiast. From the beginning of time he has been scanning the airwaves, looking for incoming messages, sifting the incoming traffic, listening for prayers. By and large they have been a muddy and indistinct lot, these ascending prayers. A bit like mine, really: faint, full of interruptions and complaints, and selfishness and petulant grumbles, and mixed motives and imperfections. 'Lord, I thank you that I am not as other men.' 'Lord, take my enemies' babies and smash their heads against the wall.' Prayers said standing up in the synagogues and at the street corners, so that people can see. Bull's blood and goat's blood, holocausts and sacrifices offered day after day, but mechanically. For centuries he's put up with this, this second-rate murmur of reluctant homage. And then one morning, as he turns the dial, a voice breaks through which is crystal clear, strong, beautiful, single-minded, unfaltering, unselfconscious, a voice which pours out a melody of adoration and joy and thanksgiving and glory so total that there is nothing more to be said by creature to Creator. It's Christ on the hillside, very early in the morning. And the Father sits back with tears in his eyes and a smile on his lips, and he says, 'At last. I know that voice. That's my boy, that's my Son in whom I am well pleased.'

That passage in Mark has a surprising content if you analyse it. It says that Jesus got up, and went out of the house, and went off to the desert place. Three verbs. Those three verbs could equally well be used of the Resurrection and Ascension of Our Lord. The Greek word for 'got up' is the same as the word for 'rose'. The 'coming out' could as easily be done from the tomb as from the house. The term for 'went off' is used to describe a journey to a place where he could find his Father, a place apart. It could equally well apply to his departure to heaven, his work accomplished. Like an arrow released from a bow, he returned unerringly to his Father's heart. Now, I don't know if Mark meant this undertone to be there, and I'm not a Scripture scholar, and I wouldn't care to argue the case. But what is true is that the perfect adoration which Jesus *spoke* to his Father on the mountainside, on this and on other occasions, he *lived* by the Paschal Mystery, by his death, resurrection and ascension.

And I am entitled to stand at the altar each day, and hold Host and Chalice in my hand, and say, 'Through him, with him and in him, in the unity of the Holy Spirit, all honour and glory is yours, almighty Father, for ever and ever.' And every time I do that, that pure, strong, flawless, accurate, passionate voice of total adoration rings out, as surely as in Mark 1:35, as surely as on Calvary and in the Garden. Adoration lived and spoken, beyond which there is nothing more to be said. Unrepeatable sacrifice enacted in my prayer-box of a 1950s church. The Paschal Mystery in its totality. And I'm part of the action.

I apply to myself what Gerard Manley Hopkins wrote.

> In a flash, at a trumpet crash,
> I am all at once what Christ is, since he was what I am and
> This Jack, joke, poor potsherd, patch, matchwood,
>   immortal diamond
> Is immortal diamond.

Personal mini-triumphs are not relevant to this.